Lectures to Young Men on Various Important Subjects

by Henry Ward Beecher

Originally published in 1845.

DEDICATION

To Lyman Beecher,

To you I owe more than to any other living being. In childhood, you were my Father; in later life, my Teacher; in manhood, my Companion. To your affectionate vigilance I owe my principles, my knowledge, and that I am a Minister of the Gospel of Christ. For whatever profit they derive from this little Book — the young will be indebted to you.

PREFACE

Having watched the courses of those who seduce the young — their arts, their blandishments, their pretenses; having witnessed the beginning and consummation of ruin, almost in the same year, of many young men, naturally well disposed, whose downfall began with the appearances of innocence; I felt an earnest desire, if I could, to warn the young, and to direct their reason to the arts by which they are, with such facility, destroyed!

I ask every young man who may read this book, not to submit his judgment to mine, not to hate because I denounce, nor blindly to follow me; but to weigh my reasons, that he may form his own judgment. I only claim the place of a friend; and that I may gain his ear, I have sought to present truth in those forms which best please the young. And though I am not without hope of satisfying the aged and the wise — my whole thought has been to carry with me the intelligent sympathy of young men.

REVIEWS

[From D. H. Allen, Professor at Lane Seminary, Cincinnati, Ohio.]

"We have a variety of books designed for young men, but I know of none worth half as much as this. It will be sure to be read, and if read, will not be easily forgotten; and the young man who reads and remembers it, will always have before him a vivid picture of the snares and pitfalls to which he is exposed. Every youth should possess it. Every father should place it in the hands of his sons. It should be in every Sabbath School Library, on board every Steamboat, in every Hotel, and wherever young men spend a leisure hour."

[From Wm. H. McGuffoy, Professor at Woodward College, Cincinnati, Ohio.]

"Mr. Beecher sketches character with a masterly hand; and the old, as well as the young, must bear witness to the truth and fidelity of his portraits. I would recommend the book to the especial attention of those for whom it was designed, and hope that the patronage extended to this may encourage the author to make other efforts through the press, for the promotion of sound morals."

[From Dr. A. Wylie, President of the Indiana University, at Bloomington.]

"The indignant rebukes which the author deals out against that spirit of licentiousness which shows itself in those frivolous works which he mentions, and which are corrupting the taste as well as the morals of our youth, have my warmest approbation. The warnings which Mr. Beecher has given on the subject of amusements are greatly needed. In short, the book deserves a place on the shelf of every household in the land, to be read by the old as well as the young!"

(From Dr. C. White, President of Wabash College, Crawfordsville, Indiana.]

"Beecher's Lectures follow a long series of elaborate and able works addressed to young men by some of our best writers. It is no small merit of this production, that it is not less instructive and impressive than the best of those which have preceded it, at the same time, that it is totally unlike them all. Mr. Beecher has given to young men most important warnings, and most valuable advice with unusual fidelity, and powerful effect. Avoiding the abstract and formal, he has pointed out to the young, the evils and advantages which surround them, with so much reality and vividness — that we almost forget we are reading a book, instead of looking personally into the interior scenes of a living and breathing community. These lectures will bear to be read often."

[From Hon. John McLean, Judge of the Supreme Court of the United States.]

"I know of no work so admirably calculated, if read with attention, to lead young men to correctness of thought and action, and I earnestly recommend it to the study of every young man who desires to become eminently respectable and useful."

[From E. W. Sehon, General Agent American Bible Society for the West]

"The intention of the author is well preserved throughout this volume. We commend the book for its boldness and originality of thought and independence of expression. The young men of our country cannot too highly appreciate the efforts of one who has thus nobly and affectionately labored for their good."

[From Pastor James H. Perkins, Cincinnati, Ohio]

"I have read Mr. Henry W. Beecher's lectures to young men with a great deal of pleasure. They appear to me to contain advice better adapted to our country, than can be found in any similar work with which I am acquainted; and this advice is presented in a style far better calculated than that common to the pulpit, to attract and please the young. I would certainly recommend the volume to any young man, as worthy of frequent perusal, and trust our American pulpit may produce many others as pleasing and practical."

[From T. E. Cressy, Pastor of the First Baptist Church, Cincinnati, Ohio.]

"There is so much ignorance among good men in general, in all our cities and large towns, of the astonishing prevalence of vice, especially of licentiousness and of its procuring causes; and there is such a false delicacy on the part of those who know these things, to hold them up to the gaze of the unsuspecting, that this book will not pass for its real worth. But it is a very valuable work. It speaks the truth in all plainness. It should be in every family library; every young man should first read and then study it!"

(From J. Blanchard, Pastor of the Fifth Presbyterian Church, Cincinnati, Ohio.]

"The book is both pleasing and profitable. It is filled with vivid sketches and delineations of vice; weighty instructions, pithy sentiments, delicate turns of thought, and playful sallies of humor! And in style and matter, is admirably adapted to the tastes and needs of the class for whom it is written."

[From T. A. Mills, Pastor of the Third Presbyterian Church, Cincinnati, Ohio.]

"The matter of this work is excellent — and the style striking and attractive. The dangers of young men are vividly portrayed, and much moral instruction given. Many of the popular vices of the present day are handled as they deserve. No young man can read the book attentively without profit, and its perusal would prove advantageous even to those who are immersed in the cares and business of life. It will need no recommendation after it becomes known."

[From the Indiana State Journal.]

"We have no doubt that these Lectures, as read, will produce a powerful impression! The pictures which glow from the hand of the artist arrest the eye — so admirable is the style and arrangement; nor will the interest once aroused slacken, until the whole sketch shall be contemplated. And the effect of the sketch — like that of a visit to the dens of iniquity shorn of their blandishments — cannot fail to be of the most wholesome warning character."

[From the Daily Cincinnati Gazette.]

"To find anything new or peculiar in a work of this kind, now-a-days, would indeed be strange. In this respect we were agreeably surprised in looking over the book before us. The subjects, though many of them are commonplace, are important and handled in a masterly manner. The author shows himself acquainted with the world, and with human nature, in all its varying phases. He writes as one who has learned the dangers and temptations that beset the young — from personal observation, and not from hearsay."

[From the Ohio State Journal, Columbus, Ohio.]

"The garb in which the author presents his subjects, makes them exceedingly attractive, and must make his Lectures very popular, when the public shall become acquainted with them. When delivered, it was not the design of the accomplished author to publish them — but at the earnest solicitation of a number of prominent citizens of Indiana, who were convinced that they would have a highly beneficial influence in arresting the progress of vice and immorality — he prepared them for the press, and they are now published in a cheap and neat form."

[From the Baptist Cross and Journal, Columbus, Ohio.]

"It is an excellent book, and should be in the hands of every young man, and of many parents. But few of those who are anxious to place their sons in large towns and cities — are aware of the temptations which beset them there; or of the many sons thus placed, who are unable to withstand these temptations. This work will open their eyes, and place them on their guard. It is written in a popular, captivating style, and is neatly printed. It goes right at the besetting sins of our age, and handles them without gloves. It ought to be extensively circulated."

[From the Cincinnati Daily Herald.]

"Mr. Beecher looks at things in his own way, and utters his thoughts in his own style. His conceptions are strong, his speech direct and to the point. The work is worthy of anybody's perusal. This book is entirely practical, and specially appropriate to the times — and its views, so far as we can speak from our own perusal, are just, and very forcible."

[From the Louisville Journal.]

"It is the most valuable addition to our youth literature that has been made for many years. Let all get it and read it carefully."

[From the 'Olive Branch']

"Beecher's Lectures To Young Men is one of the most able, interesting and really useful works for young men. Every young man should have a copy of it!"

[From the New York Commercial Advertiser.]

"The subjects are practical — such as concern all young men especially at the present day. The sentiments of the writer are put forth with much conciseness and vigor of style, for Mr. Beecher writes like one in earnest. We would wish that every young man had the book put into his hands

— especially every youth "whose avocation or choice may lead him to reside in any of the larger cities."

[From the Christian Observer, Philadelphia.]

"This is a new edition of an approved and excellent book, which it affords us pleasure to recommend to young men in every part of the country. The author's thoughts, style, and manner, are his own; and his vivid sketches of the evils which surround the young, are replete with important counsels and valuable instruction."

[From the Christian Mirror, Portland, Maine.]

"Characters and qualities, whether for warning or imitation, are drawn with uncommon graphic power and justness of delineation, as anyone may satisfy himself who will turn to 'the picture gallery,' and survey the full length portraits of the Wit, the Humorist, the Cynic, the Libertine, the Demagogue, and the Party-man. Would that every family might procure and peruse it!"

[From the Christian Citizen.]

"This is a volume of good strong Saxon thoughts, which no young man can read without thinking the like. The author talks right into the avocations of every-day life, as if he had been there himself, and were not dealing in kid glove theories of life and duty. Young men, you had better buy this book; it costs but little, and it will be worth a hundred dollars a year to you — if you read it in the right way!"

[From the Christian Reflector, Boston.]

"This is especially the 'young man's manual'. It treats of the most important subjects, with simple directness, and yet with the hand of a master. There are thousands of young men in Boston who should read it with profit and interest, and not a few whom its perusal might save from the yawning gulf of corruption and ruin! Let every young man secure this book, and read it!"

[From the Portland Transcript.]

"In handling his subjects, the author has a peculiar style. There is a freshness and originality about it, which at once arrests attention. He writes with an ungloved hand — presents truth, as truth should be presented — naked! Whatever there is beautiful, or whatever there is hideous about her — there she stands, a mark for all to gaze at! We have vices enough in New England which need rebuking and reforming. There are none so virtuous who may not be profited by these lectures. They are addressed to the young men particularly — yet the aged may glean from them many a useful lesson. We commend the work heartily to all. It is not a dry, abstract treatise on morals; but highly practical throughout. The pictures presented are life-like — flesh and blood portraits. The illustrations are apt and insightful, while an occasional vein of humor comes in as a very agreeable seasoning. The author writes like one in earnest, like one who feels the importance of the duty he has assumed. A better work for the young, we have rarely read."

[From the Daily Evening Transcript, Boston.]

"These Lectures abound in important and impressive truths, expressed in clear and pungent language. Mr. Beecher's style is remarkable for compactness and forcibleness. He occasionally thunders and lightenings, but it is to arouse young men to the dangers to which they are exposed. There is a freshness and vivacity about his thoughts and language, which must interest as well as instruct and warn the young. We desire that every young man in our city — yes, in our country — had a copy of these lectures in his hands! They can scarcely fail to interest every intelligent reader, nor to benefit every young man not lost to a sense of duty, not blind to danger, not in love with vice."

[From the Advocate of Moral Reform, New York.]

"Wherever this book is known, it is regarded of superlative worth. In our judgment no young man should enter upon city-life without it. Employers, both in city and country, should place it in the hands of their clerks and apprentices. Fathers should give it to their sons, and sons should keep it next their Bibles, and engrave its precepts upon their hearts. We are glad to learn, that, although so recently published, it has passed to a third edition, and the demand for it is increasing."

[From the Congregational Journal, Concord, N. H.]

"The writer draws his sketches with the hand of a master, and entering upon his work with a hearty interest in the young, for whom he writes it — he makes them feel that he is honest and in earnest. While the book is not lacking in seriousness — it has the charm of variety; and though it encourages solemn Christian and moral principles, the pictures drawn in it are so vivid, that it will be read with the interest of an ingenious work of fiction. Every father should read it in his family!"

Highly recommendatory notices appeared in the New York Evangelist, New York Observer, Christian World, Christian Register, Christian Watchman, etc, etc. Valuable notices have appeared in most of the papers in New England and New York state, too numerous to copy.

The Immoral Woman!

"All Scripture is God-breathed and is useful for teaching, rebuking, correcting and training in righteousness, so that the man of God may be thoroughly equipped for every good work." 2 Timothy 3:16-17

Surely one cannot declare the whole counsel of God, and leave out a subject which is interwoven with almost every chapter of the Bible. So inveterate is the prejudice against introducing into the pulpit the subject of immorality, that Ministers of the Gospel, knowing the vice to be singularly dangerous and frequent — have yet by silence almost complete, or broken only by circuitous allusions, manifested their submission to the popular taste. That Vice upon which it has pleased God to be more explicit and full, than upon any other; against which he uttered his voice upon Sinai, "You shall not commit adultery;" upon which the lawgiver, Moses, legislated with boldness; which Judges condemned; upon which the venerable Prophets spoke often and again; against which Christ with singular directness and plainness uttered the purity of religion; and upon which He inspired Paul to discourse to the Corinthians, and to almost every primitive church; this subject, upon which the Bible does not so much speak, as thunder — not by a single bolt — but peal after peal — we are solemnly warned not to introduce into the pulpit! I am entirely aware of the delicacy of introducing this subject into the pulpit.

The proverbs of Solomon are designed to furnish us a series of maxims for every relation of life. There will naturally be the most said where there is the most needed. If the frequency of warning against any sin measures the liability of man to that sin, then none is worse than Impurity. In many separate passages is the solemn warning against the immoral woman given with a force which must terrify all but the innocent or incorrigible; and with a delicacy which all will feel but those whose modesty is the fluttering of an impure imagination. I shall take such parts of all these passages as will make up a connected narrative.

When wisdom enters into your heart, and knowledge is pleasant unto your soul, discretion shall preserve you . . . to deliver you from the immoral woman, who chatters with her tongue; her lips drop as a honey-comb, her mouth is smoother than oil. She sits at the door of her house on a seat in the high places of the city, to call to passengers who go right on their ways: "Whoever is simple let him turn in here." To him that lacks understanding, she says, "Stolen waters are sweet and bread eaten in secret is pleasant;" but he knows not that the dead are there. Lust not after her beauty, neither let her capture you with her eyelids. She forsakes the guide of her youth, and forgets the covenant of her God. Remove your way far from her, and come not near the door of her house, for her house inclines unto death! She has cast down many wounded; yes, many strong men have been slain by her. Her house is the way to Hell, going down to the chamber of death; none that go unto her, return again; neither take they hold of the paths of life. Let not your heart incline to her ways, lest you mourn at last, when your flesh and your body are consumed, and say: "How have I hated instruction, and my heart despised correction!"

I. Can language be found which can draw a corrupt beauty so vividly as this? Look out upon that fallen creature whose mirthful sally through the street calls out the significant laugh of bad men, the pity of good men, and the horror of the pure. Was not her cradle as pure as ever a beloved infant? Love soothed its cries. Sisters watched its peaceful sleep, and a mother pressed it fondly to her bosom! Had you afterwards, when spring-flowers covered the earth, and every gale was fragrance, and every sound was music, seen her, fairer than the lily or the violet, searching them, would you not have said, "Sooner shall the rose grow poisonous than she; both may wither — but neither corrupt." And how often, at evening, did she clasp her tiny hands in prayer? How often did she put the wonder-raising questions to her mother, of God, and Heaven, and the dead — as if she had seen heavenly things in a vision!

As young womanhood advanced, and these foreshadowed graces ripened to the bud and burst into bloom, health glowed in her cheek, love looked from her eye, and purity was an atmosphere around her. Alas! she forsook the guide of her youth. Faint thoughts of evil, like a far-off cloud which the sunset gilds, came first; nor does the rosy sunset blush deeper along the Heaven, than her cheek, at the first thought of evil. Now, ah! mother, and you guiding elder sister, could you have seen the lurking spirit embosomed in that cloud, a holy prayer might have broken the spell, a tear have washed its stain! Alas! they saw it not; she spoke it not; she was forsaking the guide of her youth. She thinks no more of Heaven. She breathes no more prayers. She has no more penitential tears to shed; until, after a long life, she drops the bitter tear upon the cheek of despair — then her only suitor. You have forsaken the covenant of your God. Go down! fall never to rise! Hell opens to be your home!

Oh Prince of torment! if you have transforming power, give some relief to this once innocent child, whom another has corrupted! Let your deepest damnation seize him who brought her here! let his coronation be upon the very mount of torment! and the rain of fiery hail be his salutation! He shall be crowned with thorns poisoned and anguish-bearing; and every woe beat upon him, and every wave of Hell roll over the first risings of baffled hope. Your guilty thoughts, and guilty deeds, shall flit after you with bows which never break, and quivers forever emptying but never exhausted!

If Satan has one dart more poisoned than another; if God has one bolt more transfixing and blasting than another; if there is one hideous spirit more unrelenting than others — they shall be yours, most execrable wretch! who led her to forsake the guide of her youth, and to abandon the covenant of her God.

II. The next injunction of God to the young, is upon the ensnaring danger of Beauty. "Desire not her beauty in your heart, neither let her capture you with her eyelids." God did not make so much of nature with exquisite beauty, or put within us a taste for it, without an object. He meant that it should delight us. He made every flower to charm us. He never made a color, nor graceful-flying bird, nor silvery insect, without meaning to please our taste. When He clothes a man or woman with beauty — He confers a favor, did we know how to receive it. Beauty, with amiable dispositions and ripe intelligence — is more to any woman than a queen's crown. The peasant's daughter, the rustic belle, if they have woman's sound discretion, may be rightfully prouder than kings' daughters; for God adorns those who are both good and beautiful; man can only conceal the lack of beauty, by blazing jewels.

As moths and tiny insects flutter around the bright blaze which was kindled for no harm — so the foolish young, fall down burned and destroyed by the blaze of beauty. As the flame which burns to destroy the insect, is consuming itself and soon sinks into ashes — so beauty, too often, draws on itself that ruin which it inflicts upon others.

If God has given you beauty, tremble; for it is as gold in your house — thieves and robbers will prowl around and seek to possess it. If God has put beauty before your eyes, remember how many strong men have been cast down wounded by it. Are you stronger than David? Are you stronger than mighty patriarchs? — than kings and princes, who, by its fascinations, have lost peace and purity, and honor, and riches, and armies, and even kingdoms? Let other men's destruction be your wisdom and warning; for it is hard to reap prudence upon the field of experience.

III. In the minute description of this dangerous creature, mark next how seriously we are cautioned of her WILES.

Her wiles of dress. Coverings of tapestry and the fine linen of Egypt are hers; the perfumes of myrrh and aloes and cinnamon. Silks and ribbons, laces and rings, gold and equipage; ah! how low a price for damnation! The wretch who would be hung simply for the sake of riding to the gallows in a golden chariot, clothed in king's raiment — what a fool is he! Yet how many consent to enter the chariot of Death — drawn by the fiery steeds of lust which fiercely fly, and stop not for food or breath until they have accomplished their fatal journey — if they may spread their seat with flowery silks, or flaunt their forms with glowing apparel and precious jewels!

Her wiles of speech. Beasts may not speak; this honor is too high for them. To God's imaged-sons, this prerogative belongs, to utter thought and feeling in articulate sounds. We may breathe our thoughts to a thousand ears, and inspire a multitude with the best portions of our soul. How, then, has this soul's breath, this echo of our thoughts, this only image of our feelings — been perverted, that from the lips of sin it has more persuasion, than from the lips of wisdom! What horrid wizard has put the world under a spell and charm, that words from the lips of an immoral woman shall ring upon the ear like tones of music; while words from the divine lips of religion fall upon the startled ear like the funeral tones of the burial-bell! Wisdom seems crabbed; sin seems fair. Purity sounds morose; but from the lips of the harlot, words drop as honey, and flow smoother than oil; her speech is fair, her laugh is as merry as music. The eternal glory of purity has no luster — but the deep damnation of lust is made as bright as the gate of Heaven!

Her wiles of Love. Love is the mind's light and heat; it is that tenuous air in which all the other faculties exist, as we exist in the atmosphere. A mind of the greatest stature without love, is like the huge pyramid of Egypt — chill and cheerless in all its dark halls and passages. A mind with love, is as a king's palace lighted for a royal festival.

Shame! that the sweetest of all the mind's attributes should be suborned to sin! that this daughter of God should become a slave to arrogant lusts! — the cup-bearer to tyrants! — yet so it is. Devil-tempter! will your poison never cease? — shall beauty be poisoned? — shall language be charmed? — shall love be made to defile like pitch, and burn as the living coals?

Her tongue is like a bended bow, which sends the silvery shaft of flattering words. Her eyes shall cheat you, her dress shall beguile you, her beauty is a trap, her sighs are baits, her words are lures, her love is poisonous, her flattery is the spider's web spread for you. Oh! trust not your heart nor ear with Delilah! The locks of the mightiest Samson are soon shorn off, if he will but lay his slumbering head upon her lap. He who could slay heaps upon heaps of Philistines, and bear upon his huge shoulders the ponderous iron-gate, and pull down the vast temple — was yet too weak to contend with one wicked artful woman! Trust the sea with your tiny boat, trust the fickle wind, trust the changing skies of April, trust the miser's generosity, the tyrant's mercy; but ah! simple man, trust not yourself near the artful woman, armed in her beauty, her cunning clothing, her dimpled smiles, her sighs of sorrow, her look of love, her voice of flattery — for if you had the strength of ten Ulysses, unless God helps you — "Her house is a highway to Hell, leading down to the chambers of death!"

Next beware the wile of her reasonings. "To him who lacks understanding she says, stolen waters are sweet, and bread eaten in secret is pleasant. I came forth to meet you, and I have found you."

What says she in the credulous ear of inexperience? Why, she tells him that sin is safe; she swears to him that sin is pure; she protests to him that sin is innocent. Out of history she will entice him, and say: What king have I not sought? What conqueror have I not conquered? Philosophers have not, in all their wisdom, learned to hate me. I have been the guest of the world's greatest men. The

Egyptian priest, the Athenian sage, the Roman censor, the crude Gaul — have all worshiped in my temple. Are you afraid to tread where Plato trod, and the pious Socrates? Are you wiser than all that ever lived?

Nay, she reads the Bible to him; she goes back along the line of history, and reads of Abraham, and of his glorious compeers; she skips past Joseph with averted looks, and reads of David and of Solomon; and whatever chapter tells how good men stumbled, there she has turned down a leaf, and will persuade you, with honeyed speech, that the best deeds of good men were their sins; and that you should only imitate them in their stumbling and falls!

Or, if the Bible will not cheat you, how will she plead your own nature; how will she whisper, "God has made you so!" How, like her father Adam, will she lure you to pluck the apple, saying, "You shall not surely die!" And she will hiss at virtuous men, and spit on modest women, and shake her serpent-tongue at any purity which shall keep you from her ways. Oh! then, listen to what God says: "With much fair speech she causes him to yield; with the flattery of her lips she forced him. He goes after her as an ox goes to slaughter, or as a fool to the correction of the stocks, until a dart strike through his liver — as a bird hastens to a snare, and knows not that it is for his life!"

I will point only to another wile. When inexperience has been beguiled by her infernal machinations, how, like a flock of startled birds, will spring up late regrets, and shame, and fear. And worst of all, how will conscience ply her scorpion-whip and lash you, uttering with stern visage, "you are dishonored, you are a wretch, you are lost!" When the soul is full of such outcry, memory cannot sleep; she wakes, and while conscience still plies the scourge, will bring back to your thoughts, youthful purity, home, a mother's face, a sister's love, a father's counsel. Perhaps it is out of the high Heaven that your mother looks down to see your baseness. Oh! if she has a mother's heart — nay — but she cannot weep for you there!

These wholesome pains, not to be felt if there were not yet health in the mind, would save the victim, could they have time to work. But how often have I seen the spider watch, from his dark round hole, the struggling fly, until he began to break his web; and then dart out to cast his long lithe arms about him, and fasten new cords stronger than ever! So, God says, the immoral woman shall secure her ensnared victims, if they struggle. Lest you should ponder the path of life, her ways are changeable that you can not know them.

She is afraid to see you soberly thinking of leaving her, and entering the path of life; therefore her ways are changeable. She multiplies devices, she studies a thousand new wiles, she has some sweet word for every sense — lust for your pride, praise for your vanity, generosity for your selfishness, religion for your conscience, racy quips for your wearisomeness, spicy scandal for your curiosity. She is never still, nor the same; but evolving as many shapes as the rolling cloud, and as many colors as dress the wide prairie.

IV. Having disclosed her wiles, let me show you what God says of the chances of ESCAPE to those who once follow her: "None who go to her return, or attain the paths of life!" The strength of this language was not meant absolutely to exclude hope from those who, having wasted their substance in riotous living, would yet return; but to warn the unfallen, into what an almost hopeless gulf they plunge, if they venture. Some may escape — as here and there a mangled sailor crawls out of the water upon the beach — the only one or two of the whole crew; the rest are gurgling in the waves with impotent struggles, or already sunk to the bottom!

There are many evils which hold their victims by the force of habit; there are others which fasten them, by breaking their return to society. Many a person never reforms, because reform would bring no relief. There are other evils which hold men to them, because they are like the beginning of a fire; they tend to burn with fiercer and wider flames, until all fuel is consumed, and go out only when there is nothing to burn! Of this last kind is the sin of immorality: and when the conflagration once breaks out, experience has shown, what the Bible long ago declared — that the chances of reformation are few indeed. The certainty of continuance is so great, that the chances of escape are dropped from the calculation; and it is said roundly, "None who go unto her, return again!"

V. We are repeatedly warned against the immoral woman's house. There is no vice like immorality, to delude with the most fascinating offers of delight — and fulfill the promise with the most loathsome experience. All vices at the beginning, are silver-tongued — but none so impassioned as this. All vices in the end, cheat their dupes — but none with such overwhelming disaster as immorality. I shall describe by an allegory . . .

    its specious seductions;
    its plausible promises;
    its apparent innocence;

its delusive safety;

its deceptive joys — their change, their sting, their flight, their misery;

and the victim's ruin!

HER HOUSE has been cunningly planned by an Evil Architect to attract and please the attention. It stands in a vast garden full of enchanting objects. It shines in glowing colors, and seems full of happiness and full of pleasure. All the signs are of unbounded enjoyment — safe, if not innocent. Though every beam is rotten, and the house is the house of death, and in it are all the vicissitudes of infernal misery; yet to the young, it appears like a palace of delight. They will not believe that death and damnation can lurk behind so brilliant a fabric. Those who are within, look out and pine to return; and those who are without, look in and pine to enter. Such is the mastery of deluding sin.

That part of the garden which borders on the highway of innocence, is carefully planted. There is not a poison-weed, nor thorn, nor thistle there. Ten thousand flowers bloom, and waft a thousand fragrances. A victim cautiously inspects it; but it has been too carefully patterned upon innocency, to be easily detected. This outer garden is innocent — innocence is the lure to wile you from the right path, into her grounds — innocence is the bait of that trap by which she has secured all her victims.

At the gate stands a lovely porter, welcoming kindly: "Whoever is simple, let him turn in here!" Will the youth enter? Will he seek her house? To himself he says, "I will enter only to see the garden — its fruits, its flowers, its birds, its arbors, its warbling fountains!" He is resolved in virtue. He seeks wisdom, not sinful pleasure! — Dupe! you are deceived already! And this is your first lesson of wisdom.

He passes, and the porter leers behind him! He is within an Enchanter's garden! Can he not now return, if he wishes? — he will not wish to return, until it is too late. He ranges the outer garden near to the highway, thinking as he walks: "How foolishly have I been alarmed at pious lies about this beautiful place! I heard it was Hell — I find it is Paradise!"

Emboldened by the innocency of his first steps, he explores the garden further from the road. The flowers grow richer; their fragrances exhilarate; the very fruit breathes perfume like flowers; and birds seem intoxicated with delight among the fragrant shrubs and loaded trees. Soft and silvery music steals along the air. "Are angels singing? — Oh! fool that I was, to fear this place — it is all the Heaven I need! Ridiculous minister, to tell me that death was here — where all is beauty, fragrance, and melody! Surely, death never lurked in so gorgeous apparel as this! Death is grim and hideous!"

He has now come near to the immoral woman's house. If it was beautiful from afar — it is celestial now; for his eyes are bewitched with magic. When our passions enchant us — how beautiful is the way to death! In every window are sights of pleasure; from every opening, issue sounds of joy — the lute, the harp, bounding feet, and echoing laughter. Nymphs have spotted this pilgrim of temptation — they smile and beckon him. Where are his resolutions now? This is the virtuous youth who came only to observe! He has already seen too much! But he will see more; he will taste, feel, regret, weep, wail, and die!

The most beautiful nymph that eye ever rested on, approaches with decent guise and modest gestures, to give him hospitable welcome. For a moment he recalls his home, his mother, his sister-circle; but they seem far-away, dim, powerless! Into his ear, the beautiful herald pours the sweetest sounds of love: "You are welcome here, and worthy! You have great wisdom, to break the bounds of superstition, and to seek these grounds where summer never ceases, and sorrow never comes! Hail! and welcome to the House of Pleasure!"

There seemed to be a response to these words — the house, the trees, and the very air, seemed to echo, "Hail! and welcome!" In the stillness which followed, had the victim been less intoxicated, he might have heard a clear and solemn voice which seemed to fall straight down from Heaven: "Do not come near the door of her house. Her house is the way to Hell, going down to the chambers of death!"

It is too late! He has gone in — and shall never return. He goes after her immediately, as an ox goes to the slaughter; or as a fool to the correction of the stocks — and knows not that it is for his life!

Enter with me, in imagination, the immoral woman's house — where, God grant you may never enter in any other way. There are five rooms — Pleasure, Satiety, Reality, Disease, and Damnation.

1. The Room of PLEASURE. The eye is dazzled with the magnificence of its apparel — soft velvet, glossy silks, burnished satins, crimson draperies, plushy carpets. Exquisite pictures glow upon the walls, carved marble adorns every niche. The inhabitants deceive by these lying

shows; they dance, they sing; with beaming eyes they utter softest strains of flattery and graceful compliment. They partake the amorous wine, and the feast which loads the table. They eat, they drink, they are blithe and merry.

Surely, they should be happy; for after this brief hour, they shall never know purity nor joy again! For this moment's revelry — they are selling their soul and Heaven! The immoral woman walks among her guests in all her charms; fans the flame of joy, scatters grateful fragrances, and urges on the fatal revelry. As her poisoned wine is quaffed, and the mirthful creatures begin to reel, the torches wane and cast but a twilight. One by one, the guests grow somnolent; and, at length, they all repose. Their cup is exhausted, their pleasure is forever over — life has exhaled to a vapor, and that is consumed! While they sleep, servants, practiced to the work — and remove them all to another room.

2. The Room of SATIETY. An excess of sensual gratification — excites wearisomeness or loathing! Here reigns a bewildering twilight through which can hardly be discerned the wearied inhabitants — yet sluggish upon their couches.

Over-flushed with dance, sated with wine and sweets — a fitful drowsiness vexes them. They wake — to crave; they taste — to loathe; they sleep — to dream; they wake again from unquiet visions. They long for the sharp taste of pleasure — so grateful yesterday. Again they sink, repining to sleep; by starts, they rouse at an ominous dream; by starts, they hear strange cries! The sweets burn and torment; the wine shoots sharp pains through their body. Strange wonder fills them. They remember the recent joy — as a reveler in the morning thinks of his midnight madness. The glowing garden and the sumptuous banquet now seem all stripped and gloomy. They meditate return; pensively they long for their native spot! At sleepless moments, mighty resolutions form — as substantial as a dream. Memory grows dark. Hope will not shine.

> The past is not pleasant!
> The present is wearisome!
> And the future is gloomy!

3. The Room of REALITY. In the third room, no deception remains.

> The floors are bare;
> the naked walls drip filth;
> the air is poisonous with sickly fumes, and echoes with mirth concealing hideous misery!

None supposes that he has been happy. The past seems like the dream of the miser, who gathers gold spilled like rain upon the road, and awakes, clutching his bed, and crying "Where is it?"

On your right hand, as you enter, close by the door, is a group of fierce felons in deep drink with drugged liquor. With red and swollen faces; or white and thin; or scarred with ghastly corruption; with scowling brows, malevolent eyes, bloated lips and demoniac grins — in person all filthy, in morals all debauched, in peace, bankrupt. The desperate wretches wrangle one with the other, swearing bitter oaths, and heaping reproaches each upon each!

Around the room you see miserable creatures unclothed, or dressed in rags — sobbing and moaning.

That one who gazes out at the window, calling for her mother and weeping — was rightly, tenderly, and purely bred. She has been baptized twice — once to God, and once to the Devil! She sought this place in the very vestments of God's house. "Do not call upon your mother! She is a saint in Heaven, and cannot hear you!" Yet, all night long she dreams of home, and childhood, and wakes to sigh and weep; and between her sobs, she cries "Mother! mother!"

Yonder is another youth, once a servant at God's house. His hair hangs tangled and torn; his eyes are bloodshot; his face is ashen; his fist is clenched. All the day, he wanders up and down, cursing sometimes himself, and sometimes the wretch that brought him here! And when he sleeps — he dreams of Hell; and then he awakes to feel all he dreamed!

This is the Room of Reality. All know why the first rooms looked so gay — they were enchanted! It was enchanted wine they drank; and enchanted fruit they ate! Now they know the pain of fatal poison in every limb!

4. The Room of DISEASE. You who look wistfully at the pleasant front of this lovely house — come with me now, and look long into the terror of this room; for here are the seeds of sin in their full harvest form! We are in a leper-room!

> Its air disgusts every sense;
> its sights confound our thoughts;
> its sounds appall our ear;
> its stench repels us;
> it is full of diseases!

Here a shuddering wretch is clawing at his breast — to tear away that worm which gnaws his heart!

By him, is another wretch, whose limbs are dropping from his ghastly trunk.

Next, swelters another wretch in reeking filth — his eyes rolling in bony sockets, every breath a pang, and every pang a groan!

But yonder, on a pile of rags, lies one whose yells of frantic agony appall every ear! Clutching his rags with spasmodic grasp, his swollen tongue lolling from a blackened mouth, his bloodshot eyes glaring and rolling — he shrieks curses; now blaspheming God — and now imploring him. He hoots and shouts, and shakes his grisly head from side to side, cursing or praying; now calling death, and then, as if driving away fiends, abhorrently yelling, "Get away! Be gone!"

Another has been ridden by pain, until he can no longer shriek; but lies foaming and grinding his teeth, and clenches his bony hands, until the finger-nails pierce the palm — though there is no blood there to flow out — trembling all the time with the shudders and chills of utter agony.

The happiest wretch in all this room, is an Idiot — confused, distorted, and moping! All day, he wags his head, and chatters, and laughs, and bites his nails! Then he will sit for hours motionless, with open jaw, and glassy eye fixed on nothing at all.

In this room are huddled all the Diseases of Immoral Pleasure. This is the torture-room of the immoral woman's house, and it exceeds the Catholic Inquisition. The wheel, the rack; the bed of knives, the roasting-fire, the brazen-room slowly heated, the slivers driven under the finger-nails, the hot pincers — what are these tortures of the Inquisition — compared to the agonies of the last days of immoral vice? Hundreds of rotting wretches would change their couch of torment in the immoral woman's house — for the gloomiest terror of the Inquisition — and profit by the change!

Nature herself becomes the tormentor. Nature, long trespassed on and abused, at length casts down the wretch; searches every vein, makes a road of every nerve for the scorching feet of pain to travel on, pulls at every muscle, breaks in the breast, builds fires in the brain, eats out the skin, and casts living coals of torment on the heart!

What are hot pincers — compared to the envenomed claws of disease? What is it to be put into a pit of snakes and slimy toads, and feel their cold coil or piercing fang — compared to the creeping of a whole body of vipers? — where every nerve is a viper, and every vein a viper, and every muscle a serpent; and the whole body, in all its parts, coils and twists upon itself in unimaginable anguish?

I tell you, there is no Inquisition so bad, as that which the Doctor looks upon! Young man! I can show you in this room, worse pangs than ever a savage produced at the stake! — than ever a tyrant wrung out by engines of torment! — than ever an Inquisitor devised! Every year, in every town — immoral wretches die scalded and scorched with agony. Were the sum of all the pain that comes with the last stages of immorality collected — it would rend the very heavens with its outcry; it would shake the earth; it would even blanch the cheek of Infatuation!

You who are listening in the garden of this immoral woman, among her cheating flowers; you who are dancing in her halls in the first room — come here! Look upon her fourth room — its vomited blood, its sores and fiery blotches, its purulence, and rotten bones! Stop, young man! You turn your head from this ghastly room; and yet, stop! — and stop soon — or you shall soon lie here yourself! Mark the solemn signals of your passage! You have had already enough of warnings in your cheek, in your bosom, in your pangs of forewarning!

But ah! Every one of you who are dancing in the immoral woman's first hall — let me break your spell; for now I shall open the doors of the last room. Look! Listen! Witness your own end, unless you take quickly a warning!

5. The Room of DAMNATION! No longer does the incarnate wretch pretend to conceal her cruelty. She thrusts — yes! as if they were dirt — she shovels out the wretches. Some fall headlong through the rotten floor — a long fall to a fiery bottom! The floor trembles to deep thunders which roll below. Here and there, jets of flame sprout up, and give a ghastly light to the murky hall. Some would gladly escape; and flying across the treacherous floor, which man never safely passed, they go through pitfalls and treacherous traps — with hideous outcries and astounding yells — to eternal perdition! Fiends laugh! The infernal laugh! The cry of agony, the thunder of damnation — shake the very roof and echo from wall to wall.

Oh! that the young might see the end of immorality — before they see the beginning! I know that you shrink from this picture; but your safety requires that you should look long into the Room of Damnation — that fear may supply strength to your virtue. See the blood oozing from the wall, the fiery hands which pluck the wretches down, the light of Hell gleaming through, and hear its roar as of a distant ocean chafed with storms!

Will you sprinkle the wall with your blood?

Will you feed those flames with your flesh?

Will you add your voice to those thundering wails?

Will you go down a prey through the fiery floor of the chamber of damnation?

Believe then the word of God: "Her house is the way to Hell, going down to the chambers of death! Avoid it, pass not by it, turn from it, and go on your way!"

I have described the immoral woman's house in strong language — and it needed it. If your taste shrinks from the description — so does mine. Hell, and all the ways of Hell — when we pierce through the cheating disguises and see the truth — are terrible to behold! And if men would not walk there — neither would we pursue their steps. We wish to sound the alarm, and gather back whom we can!

Allow me to close, by directing your attention to a few points of especial danger.

I. I solemnly warn you against indulging a sensual imagination. In that busy and mischievous faculty, begins the evil. Were it not for his evil imaginations, man might stand his own master — not overmatched by the worst part of himself. But ah! these summer-reveries, these venturesome dreams, these fairy-castles — built for no good purposes — they are haunted by impure spirits, who will fascinate, bewitch, and corrupt you! Blessed are the pure in heart. Blessed are you, most favored of God, whose thoughts are pure; whose imagination will not breathe or fly in tainted air; and whose path has been measured by the Golden Rod of Purity.

May I not paint PURITY, as a saintly virgin, in spotless white, walking with open face, in an air so clear that no vapor can stain it? Her steps are a queen's steps; God is her father, and you her brother — if you will make her yours! Let your heart be her dwelling. Wear her ring upon your hand — and her charm on your heart.

II. Next to evil imaginations, I warn the young of evil companions. Decaying fruit corrupts the neighboring fruit. You cannot make your head a metropolis of base stories, the ear and tongue a highway of immodest words — and yet be pure. Another, as well as yourself — may throw a spark on the gun-powder of your passions — beware how your companions do it! No man is your friend who will corrupt you. An impure man is every godly man's enemy — your deadly foe; and all the worse, if he hides his poisoned dagger under the cloak of friendship. Therefore, select your associates, assort them, winnow them. Keep the grain — and let the wind sweep away the chaff.

III. But I warn you, with yet more solemn emphasis — against Evil Books and Evil Pictures! There is in every town an under-current which glides beneath our feet, unsuspected by the pure; out of which, notwithstanding, our sons scoop many a poisoned goblet. Books are hidden in trunks, concealed in dark holes; pictures are stored in sly portfolios, or trafficked from hand to hand; and the handiwork of depraved art is seen in forms which ought to make a harlot blush!

I would think a man would loathe himself, and wake up from owning such things, as from a horrible nightmare! Those who circulate them — are incendiaries of all morality! And those who make them — are the worst public criminals! A pure heart would shrink from these abominable things — as from death itself!

France, where true religion long ago was extinguished, smothered in immorality — has flooded the world with a species of literature redolent of the vilest depravity. Upon the plea of exhibiting human nature — novels are now scooped out of the very lava of corrupt passions. They are true to nature — but to nature as it exists in grossly vile and immoral hearts. Under a plea of reality — we have shown to us, troops of harlots — to prove that they are not so bad as purists think; and gangs of desperadoes — to show that there is nothing in crime inconsistent with the noblest feelings. We have in French and English, novels of the infernal school — humane murderers, lascivious saints, upright infidels, honest robbers. The devotion of these artists, is such as might be expected from vile thieves, in the vortex of thrice-deformed vice.

Obscene libertines are now our professors of morality. They scrape the very sediment and muck of society — to mold their creations; and their books are monster-galleries, in which the inhabitants of old Sodom would have felt at home as connoisseurs.

Over loathsome women, and unutterably vile men, huddled together in motley groups, and over all their monstrous deeds — their lies, their plots, their crimes, their horrendous pleasures, their appalling conversation — is thrown the impure light of a sensual imagination — until they glow with an infernal luster!

Such novels are the common-sewers of society, into which drain the concentrated filth of the worst passions, of the worst creatures, of the worst cities! Such novels come to us impudently pretending to be reformers of morals, and liberalizers of religion; they propose to instruct our laws, and teach justice to a discreet humanity!

The Ten Plagues have visited our literature: water is turned to blood; frogs and lice creep and hop over our most familiar things — the couch, the cradle, and the bread-box; locusts, plague, and fire — are smiting every green thing. I am ashamed and outraged, when I think that wretches could be found to open these foreign seals — and let out their plagues upon us — that any Satanic pilgrim should voyage to France to dip from the dead sea of her abomination — such immoral filth for our children.

It were a mercy compared to this, to import . . .
venomous serpents from Africa — and pour them out in our homes;
ferocious lions — and free them in our towns;
poisonous lizards and scorpions and black tarantulas — and put them in our gardens!
Men could slay these — but those offspring-reptiles of the French mind — who can kill these? You might as well draw sword on a plague — or charge malaria with the bayonet!

This black smut-lettered literature circulates in our towns, floats in our stores, nestles in the shops, is fingered and read nightly, and hatches broods of obscene thoughts in the young mind! While the parent strives to infuse Christian purity into his child's heart — he is checked by most accursed messengers of evil; and the child's heart hisses already like a nest of young and nimble vipers!

IV. Once more, let me persuade you that no examples in high places — can justify imitation in low places. Your purity is too precious to be bartered, because an official rogue tempts by his example! I wish that every eminent place of state were a sphere of purity and light, from which should be flung down on your path a cheering glow to guide you on to virtue. But if these wandering stars, reserved I do believe for final blackness of darkness, wheel their malignant spheres in the orbits of corruption — do not follow after them! God is greater than wicked great men; Heaven is higher than the highest places of nations; and if God and Heaven are not brighter to your eyes than great men in high places — then you must take part in their doom, when, before long, God shall dash them to pieces!

V. Let me beseech you, lastly, to guard your heart-purity. Never lose it! If it is gone — you have lost from the casket the most precious gift of God. The first purity of imagination, of thought, and of feeling, if soiled — can be cleansed by no fuller's soap. If lost — it cannot be found, though sought carefully with tears! If a harp is broken — it may be repaired; if a light is quenched — the flame may enkindle it; but if a flower is crushed — what art can repair it? If an fragrance is wafted away — who can collect or bring it back?

The heart of youth is a wide prairie. Over it hang the clouds of Heaven, to water it; and the sun throws its broad sheets of light upon it, to awake its life. Out of its bosom spring, the long season through, flowers of a hundred names and hues, entwining together their lovely forms, wafting to each other a grateful fragrance, and nodding each to each in the summer-breeze. Oh! such would man be — did he sustain that purity of heart which God gave him!

But you now have a Depraved Heart. It is a vast continent; on it are mountain-ranges of evil powers, and dark deep streams, and pools, and morasses. If once the full and terrible clouds of temptation settle thick and fixedly upon you, and begin to cast down their dreadful stores — may God save whom man can never! Then the heart shall feel tides and streams of irresistible power, mocking its control, and hurrying fiercely down from steep to steep, with growing desolation. Your only resource is to avoid the uprising of your giant-passions.

We are drawing near to Christmas day, by the usage of ages, consecrated to celebrate the birth of Christ. At his advent, God hung out a prophet-star in the Heaven; guided by it, the wise men journeyed from the east and worshiped at his feet. Oh! let the star of Purity hang out to your eye, brighter than the orient orb to the Magi; let it lead you, not to the Babe — but to His feet who now stands in Heaven, a Prince and Savior! If you have sinned — one look, one touch, shall cleanse you while you are worshiping, and you shall rise up healed.

The Portrait Gallery

"My son, if sinners entice you — do not consent!" Proverbs 1:10

He who is allured to embrace evil under some engaging form of beauty, or seductive appearance of good — is enticed. A man is tempted to what he knows to be sinful; he is enticed where the evil appears to be innocent. The Enticer wins his way by . . .

> bewildering the moral sense,
> setting false lights in the imagination,
> painting disease with the hues of health,
> making impurity to glow like innocency,
> strewing the broad-road with flowers,
> lulling its travelers with soothing music,
> hiding all its chasms,
> covering its pitfalls, and
> closing its long perspective with the mimic glow of

Paradise.

The young are seldom tempted to outright wickedness; evil comes to them as an enticement. The honest generosity and fresh heart of youth, would revolt from open baseness and undisguised vice. The Adversary conforms his wiles to their nature.

He tempts them to the basest deeds — by beginning with innocent ones, gliding to more objectionable ones, and finally, to positively wicked ones. All our warnings then must be against the spring beauty of vice. Its autumn and winter — none wish. It is my purpose to describe the enticement of particular men upon the young.

Every youth knows that there are dangerous men abroad who would injure him by lying, by slander, by over-reaching and plundering him. From such, they have little to fear, because they are upon their guard. Few imagine that they have anything to dread from those who have no designs against them; yet such is the instinct of imitation, so insensibly does the example of men steal upon us and warp our conduct to their likeness — that the young often receive a deadly injury from men with whom they never spoke! Our thoughts, our tastes, our emotions, our partialities, our prejudices, and finally, our conduct and habits — are insensibly changed by the silent influence of men who never once directly tempted us, or even knew the effect which they produced. I shall draw for your inspection, some of those dangerous men, whose open or silent enticement has availed against thousands, and will be exerted upon thousands more.

I. The WIT. It is sometimes said by morose theologians, that Christ never laughed — but often wept. I shall not quarrel with the assumption. I only say that men have within them a faculty of mirthfulness which God created. I suppose it was meant for use. Those who do not feel the impulsion of this faculty, are not the ones to sit in judgment upon those who do. It would be very absurd for an owl in an ivy bush, to read lectures on optics to an eagle; or for a mole to counsel a lynx on the sin of sharp-sightedness.

He is divinely favored, who may trace a silver vein in all the affairs of life; see sparkles of light in the gloomiest scenes; and absolute radiance in those which are bright. There are in the clouds ten thousand inimitable forms and hues, to be found nowhere else; there are in plants and trees beautiful shapes and endless varieties of color; there are in flowers minute pencilings of exquisite shades; in fruits a delicate bloom — like a veil, making the face of beauty more beautiful. Sporting among the trees, and upon the flowers, are tiny insects — gems which glow like living diamonds. Ten thousand eyes stare fully upon these things — and see nothing at all; and yet thus the Divine Artist has finished his matchless work!

Thus, too, upon all the labors of life, the events of each hour, the course of good or evil; upon each action, or word, or attitude; upon all the endless changes transpiring among myriad men — there is a delicate grace, or bloom, or sparkle, or radiance — which catches the eye of Wit, and delights it with appearances which are to the weightier matters of life — what fragrance, colors, and symmetry are, to the marketable and commercial properties of matter.

A mind imbued with this feeling is full of dancing motes, such as we see moving in sunbeams when they pour through some shutter into a dark room; and when the sights and conceptions of wit are uttered in words, they diffuse upon others that pleasure whose brightness shines upon its own cheerful imagination.

It is not strange that the Wit is a universal favorite. All companies rejoice in his presence, watch for his words, repeat his language. He moves like a comet whose incomings and outgoings are uncontrollable. He astonishes the regular stars with the eccentricity of his orbit, and flirts his long tail athwart the heavens without the slightest misgivings that it will be troublesome, and romances the very sun with audacious familiarity.

When wit is unperverted, it . . .
lightens labor,
makes the very face of care to shine,
diffuses cheerfulness among men,
multiplies the sources of harmless enjoyment,
gilds the dark things of life, and
heightens the luster of the brightest.

When wit is perverted, it . . .
becomes an instrument of malevolence,
gives a deceitful coloring to vice,
reflects a semblance of truth upon error,
and distorts the features of real truth, by false lights.

The Wit is liable . . .
to indolence — by relying upon his genius;
to vanity — by the praise which is offered as incense;
to malignant sarcasm — to revenge his affronts;
to dissipation — from the habit of exhilaration, and from the company which courts him.

The mere Wit is only a human bauble. He is to life what bells are to horses, not expected to draw the load — but only to jingle while the horses draw.

The young often repine at their own native dullness; and since God did not choose to endow them with this shining quality — they will make it for themselves. Forthwith, they are smitten with the itch of imitation. Their ears purvey to their mouth the borrowed jest; their eyes note the Wit's manner — and the awkward youth clumsily apes, in a side circle . . .

the Wit's deft and graceful gesture,
the smooth smile,

the roguish twinkle,
the sly look.

Every community is supplied with self-made Wits. One retails other men's sharp witticisms. Another roars over his own brutal quotations. Another invents a witticism by a logical deduction of circumstances, and sniffs and giggles over the result as delightfully as if other men laughed too. Other self-made Wits lie in wait around your conversation, to trip up some word, or strike a light out of some sentence. Others fish in dictionaries for pitiful puns — and all fulfill the prediction of Isaiah: "You shall conceive chaff — and bring forth stubble!"

It becomes a mania. Each school has its allusions, each circle has its apish motion, each companionhood its stock of wit-artillery. We find street-wit, shop-wit, school-wit, fool's-wit, whisky-wit, business-wit, and almost every kind of wit — but mother-wit. We find puns, quibbles, catches, would-be jests, thread-bare stories, and gew-gaw tinsel — everything but the real diamond — which sparkles simply because God made it so that it could not help sparkling. Real, native wit, is like a pleasant rill which quietly wells up in some verdant nook, and steals out from among reeds and willows noiselessly, and is seen far down the meadow, as much by the fruitfulness of its edges in flowers, as by its own glimmering light.

Let everyone beware of the insensible effect of witty men upon him! The perverted wit gild lies — so that base coin may pass for true. That which is grossly wrong — wit may make fascinating. When no argument could persuade you — the coruscations of wit may dazzle and blind you. When duty presses you — the threatenings of this human lightning may make you afraid to do right.

Remember that the very best office of wit, is only to lighten the serious labors of life; that it is only a torch, by which men may cheer the gloom of a dark way. When it sets up to be your Counselor or your guide — it is the fool's fire, flitting irregularly and leading you into the quagmire or morass. The great Dramatist represents a witty fairy to have put an donkey's head upon a man's shoulders; beware that you do not let this mischievous fairy put an ape's head upon yours!

If God has not given you this quicksilver — no art can make it; nor need you regret it. The stone, the wood, and the iron are a thousand times more valuable to society — than pearls and diamonds and rare gems. And sterling common-sense, and industry, and integrity — are better a thousand times, in the hard work of living, than the brilliance of Wit.

II. The HUMORIST. I do not employ the term to designate one who indulges in that pleasantest of all wit — inherent wit; but to describe a creature who conceals a coarse animalism under a brilliant, jovial exterior. The dangerous humorist answers very well to the Psalmist's description: "Therefore pride is their necklace; they clothe themselves with violence. From their callous hearts comes iniquity; the evil conceits of their minds know no limits. They scoff, and speak with malice." Whatever is pleasant in ease, whatever is indulgent in morals, whatever is solacing in luxury — the jovial few, the convivial many, the glass, the cards, the revel, and midnight uproar — these are his delights. His manners are easy and agreeable; his face redolent of fun and good nature; his whole air that of a man fond of the utmost possible bodily refreshment.

Withal, he is sufficiently circumspect and secretive of his course, to maintain a place in genteel society; for that is a luxury. He is not a glutton — but a choice eater. He is not a gross drinker, only a gentlemanly consumer of every curious compound of liquor. He has traveled; he can tell you which, in every city, is the best bar, the best restaurant, the best motel. He knows every theater, each actor; particularly is he versed in the select morsels of the scandalous indulgence peculiar to each. He knows every race-course, the history of all the famous matches, and the pedigree of every distinguished horse. The whole vocabulary of pleasure is vernacular — its wit, its slang, its watchwords, and blackletter literature. He is a profound annalist of scandal; every stream of news, clear or muddy, disembogues into the gulf of his prodigious memory. He can tell you, after living but a week in a city, who gambles, when, for what sums, and with what fate; who is impure, who was, who is suspected, who is not suspected — but ought to be. He is a morbid anatomist of morals; a brilliant flesh-fly — unerring to detect taint.

Like other men, he loves admiration and desires to extend his influence. All these manifold accomplishments are exhibited before the naive young. That he may secure a train of useful followers, he is profuse of money; and moves among them with an easy, insinuating frankness, a never-ceasing gaiety, so spicy with fun, so diverting with stories, so full of little hits, sly innuendoes, or solemn wit, with now and then a rare touch of dexterous mimicry, and the whole so pervaded by the indescribable flavor, the changing hues of humor — that the young are bewildered with idolatrous admiration.

What mirthful young man, who is old enough to admire himself and be ashamed of his parents, can resist a man so bedewed with humor, narrating exquisite stories with such mock gravity, with such slyness of mouth, and twinkling of the eye, with such grotesque attitudes, and significant gestures? He is declared to be the most remarkable man in the world. Now take off this man's dress, put out the one faculty of mirthfulness, and he will stand disclosed without a single positive virtue! With strong appetites deeply indulged, hovering perpetually upon the twilight edge of every vice; and whose wickedness is only not apparent, because it is garnished with flowers and garlands; who is not despised, only because his various news, artfully told, keep us in good humor with ourselves!

At one period of youthful life, this creature's influence supplants that of every other man. There is an absolute fascination in him which awakens a craving in the mind to be of his circle; plain duties become drudgery, home has no light; life at its ordinary key is monotonous, and must be screwed up to the concert pitch of this wonderful genius! As he tells his stories, so with a wretched grimace of imitation, apprentices will try to tell them; as he gracefully swings through the street, they will roll; they will leer because he stares genteelly; he sips, they guzzle — and talk impudently, because he talks with easy confidence. He walks erect, they strut; he lounges, they loll; he is less than a man, and they become even less than he.

Copper-rings, huge blotches of breastpins, wild streaming handkerchiefs, jaunty hats, odd clothes, superfluous walking-sticks, ill-uttered oaths, stupid jokes, and blundering pleasantries — these are the first fruits of imitation! There are various grades of it, from the office, store, shop, street, clear down to the stable. Our cities are filled with these juvenile nondescript monsters, these compounds of vice, low wit, and vulgarity. The original is morally detestable, and the counterfeit is a very base imitation of a very base thing; the dark shadow of a very ugly substance.

III. The Cynic. The Cynic is one who never sees a good quality in a man — and never fails to see a bad one. He is the human owl, vigilant in darkness — and blind to light; mousing for vermin — and never seeing noble game. The Cynic puts all human actions into only two classes — openly bad, and secretly bad. All virtue and generosity and unselfishness are merely the appearance of good — but selfish at the bottom. He holds that no man does a good thing, except for profit. The effect of his conversation upon your feelings, is to chill and sear them; to send you away sour and morose. His criticisms and innuendos fall indiscriminately upon every lovely thing, like frost upon flowers.

If a man is said to be pure and chaste, he will answer: "Yes, in the day-time."

If a man is pronounced virtuous, he will reply: "Yes, as yet Mr. A. is a religious man — yes, on Sundays. Mr. B. has just joined the church, certainly — the elections are coming on."

The minister of the gospel is called an example of diligence: "it is because it is his trade."

Such a man is generous: "it is of other men's money."

This man is obliging: "it is to lull suspicion and cheat you."

That man is upright: "it is because he is naive."

Thus his eye strains out every good quality — and takes in only the bad. To him . . .
religion is hypocrisy,
honesty is a preparation for fraud,
virtue is only lack of opportunity,
and undeniable purity is asceticism.

The live-long day, he will coolly sit with sneering lip, uttering sharp speeches in the quietest manner, and in polished phrase — crucifying every character which is presented. His words are softer than oil — yet are they drawn swords.

All this, to the young, seems a wonderful knowledge of human nature; they honor a man who appears to have found out mankind. They begin to indulge themselves in flippant sneers; and with supercilious brow, and impudent tongue, wagging to an empty brain — deprecate the wise, the long tried, and the venerable.

I do believe that man is corrupt enough; but something of good has survived his wreck; something of evil, religion has restrained, and something partially restored; yet, I look upon the human heart as a mountain of fire. I dread its crater. I tremble when I see its lava roll the fiery stream. Therefore, I am the more glad, if upon the old crust of past eruptions, I can find a single flower springing up. So far from rejecting appearances of virtue in the corrupt heart of a depraved race, I am eager to see their light as ever mariner was to see a star in a stormy night.

Moss will grow upon gravestones; the ivy will cling to the moldering pile; the mistletoe springs from the dying branch; and, God be praised, something green, something fair to the sight and grateful to the heart — will yet entwine around and grow out of the seams and cracks of the desolate temple of the human heart!

Who could walk through Thebes, Palmyra, or Petra, and survey the wide waste of broken arches, crumbled altars, fallen pillars, effaced cornices, toppling walls, and crushed statues, with no feelings but those of contempt? Who, unsorrowing, could see the owl's nest upon the carved pillar, satyrs dancing on marble pavements, and scorpions nestling where beauty once dwelt, and vermin the sole tenants of royal palaces? Amid such melancholy magnificence, even the misanthrope might weep! If here and there an altar stood unbruised, or a graven column unblemished, or a statue nearly perfect — he might well feel love for a man-wrought stone — so beautiful, when all else is so dreary and desolate. Thus, though man is as a desolate city, and his passions are as the wild beasts of the wilderness howling in kings' palaces — yet he is God's workmanship, and a thousand touches of exquisite beauty remain. Since Christ has put his sovereign hand to restore man's ruin, many points are remolded, and the fair form of a new fabric already appears growing from the ruins, and the first faint flame is glimmering upon the restored altar.

It is impossible to indulge in such habitual severity of opinion upon our fellow-men — without injuring the tenderness and delicacy of our own feelings. A man will be what his most cherished feelings are. If he encourages a noble generosity — every feeling will be enriched by it. If he nurses bitter and envenomed thoughts — his own spirit will absorb the poison; and he will crawl among men as a burnished adder, whose life is mischief, and whose errand is death!

Although experience should correct the indiscriminate confidence of the young, no experience should render them callous to goodness wherever seen. He who hunts for flowers — will find flowers; and he who loves weeds — may find weeds. Let it be remembered, that no man, who is not himself mortally diseased, will have a relish for disease in others. A swollen wretch, blotched all over with leprosy, may grin hideously at every wart or excrescence upon beauty. A wholesome man will be pained at it, and seek not to notice it. Reject, then, the morbid ambition of the Cynic — or cease to call yourself a man!

IV. The Libertine. I fear that few villages exist without a specimen of the Libertine. His errand into this world is to explore every depth of sensuality — and collect upon himself the foulness of every one. He is proud to be vile; his ambition is to be viler than other men. Were we not confronted almost daily by such wretches, it would be hard to believe that any could exist, to whom purity and decency were a burden — and only corruption a delight. This creature has changed his nature, until only that which disgusts a pure mind, pleases his. He is lured by the scent of carrion. His coarse feelings, stimulated by gross excitants, are insensible to delicacy. The exquisite bloom, the dew and freshness of the flowers of the heart, which delight both good men and God himself, he gazes upon, as a Behemoth would gaze enraptured upon a prairie of flowers. It is just so much pasture. The forms, the fragrances, the hues are only a mouthful for his terrible appetite.

Therefore, his breath blights every innocent thing. He sneers at the mention of purity, and leers in the very face of Virtue, as though she were herself corrupt, if the truth were known. He assures the credulous disciple that there is no purity; that its appearances are only the veils which cover indulgence. Nay, he solicits praise for the very openness of his evil; and tells the listener that all act as he acts — but only few are courageous enough to own it. But the uttermost parts of depravity are laid open, only when several such monsters meet together, and vie with each other, as we might suppose shapeless mud-monsters amuse themselves in the slimiest ooze. They dive in fierce rivalry which shall reach the most infernal depth, and bring up the blackest sediment.

It makes the blood of an honest man run cold, to hear but the echo of the shameless rehearsals of their lewd enterprises. Each strives to tell a blacker tale than the other. When the abomination of their actual life is not damnable enough to satisfy the ambition of their unutterable corruption — they devise, in their imagination, scenes yet more flagrant; swear that they have performed them, and when they separate, each strives to make his lying boastings true.

It would seem as if miscreants so loathsome, would have no power of temptation upon the young. Experience shows that the worst men are, often — the most skillful in touching the springs of human action. A young man knows little of life; less of himself. He feels in his bosom the various impulses, wild desires, restless cravings he can hardly tell for what, a somber melancholy when all is mirthful, a violent exhilaration when others are sober. These wild gushes of feeling, peculiar to youth, the sagacious tempter has felt, has studied, has practiced upon, until he can sit before that most capacious organ, the human mind, knowing every stop, and all the combinations, and competent to touch any note through the organ.

As a serpent deceived the purest of mortals — so now a beast may mislead their posterity. He begins afar off. He decries the virtue of all men; studies to produce a doubt that any are under self-restraint. He unpacks his filthy stories, plays off the fire-works of his corrupt imagination — its blue-lights, its red-lights, and green-lights, and sparkle-spitting lights; and edging in upon the yielding youth, who begins to wonder at his experience, he boasts his first exploits, he hisses at the purity of women! He grows yet bolder, tells more wicked deeds, and invents worse even than he ever performed, though he has performed worse than good men ever thought of. All thoughts, all feelings, all ambition, are merged in one — and that the lowest, vilest, most detestable ambition.

Had I a son, I could, with thanksgiving, see him go down to the grave — rather than fall into the maw of this most besotted devil. The plague is mercy, the cholera is love, the deadliest fever is refreshment to man's body — in comparison with this epitome and essence of moral disease! He lives among men as Hell's ambassador with full credentials; nor can we conceive that there should be need of any other fiend to perfect the works of darkness, while he lives among us, stuffed with every pestilent drug of corruption.

The heart of every virtuous young man should loathe him; if he speaks, you should as soon hear a wolf bark. Gather around you the venomous snake, the poisonous toad, the foul vulture, the prowling hyena — and their company would be an honor to you above his; for they at least remain within their own nature; but he goes out of his nature that he may become more vile than it is possible for a mere animal to be. He is hateful to religion, hateful to virtue, hateful to decency, hateful to the coldest morality.

The stenchful purulence of his dissolute heart, has flowed over every feeling of his nature, and left them as the burning lava leaves the garden, the orchard, and the vineyard.

And it is a wonder that the bolt of God which crushed Sodom does not slay him. It is a wonder that the earth does not refuse the burden and open and swallow him up. I do not fear that the young will be undermined by his direct assaults. But some will imitate him — and their example will be again freely imitated — and finally, a remote circle of disciples will spread the diluted contagion among the virtuous. This man will be the fountain-head, and though none will come to drink at a hot spring — yet further down along the stream it sends out, will be found many scooping from its waters.

V. The polished Libertine. I have just described the devil in his native form — but he sometimes appears as an angel of light. There is a polished Libertine, in manners studiously refined, in taste faultless; his face is mild and engaging; his words drop as pure as newly-made honey. In general society, he would rather attract regard as a model of purity, and suspicion herself could hardly look askance upon him. But under this brilliant exterior — his heart is like a sepulcher, full of all uncleanness! Contrasted with the gross libertine, it would not be supposed that he had a thought in common with him. But if his heart could be opened to our eyes, as it is to God's — we would perceive scarcely dissimilar feeling in respect to appetite. Professing unbounded admiration of virtue in general — he leaves not in private, a point untransgressed.

His reading has culled every glowing picture of amorous poets, every tempting scene of loose dramatists, and looser novelists. Enriched by these, his imagination, like a rank soil, is overgrown with a prodigal luxuriance of poison-herbs and deadly flowers.

Men such as this man is, frequently aspire to be the censors of morality. They are hurt at the injudicious reprehensions of vice from the pulpit! They make great outcry when plain words are employed to denounce base things. They are astonishingly sensitive and fearful lest good men should soil their hands with too much meddling with evil. Their cries are not the evidence of sensibility to virtue — but of too lively a sensibility to vice. Sensibility is, often, only the fluttering of an impure heart.

At the very time that their voice is ringing an alarm against immoral reformations, they are secretly skeptical of every tenet of virtue, and practically unfaithful to every one. Of these two libertines, the most refined is the more dangerous. The one is a rattlesnake which carries its warning with it; the other, hiding his burnished scales in the grass, skulks to perform unsuspected deeds in darkness. The one is the visible fog and miasma of the quagmire; the other is the serene air of a tropical city, which, though brilliant — is loaded with invisible pestilence.

The Politician. If there be a man on earth whose character should be framed of the most sterling honesty, and whose conduct should conform to the most scrupulous morality, it is the man who administers public affairs. The most romantic notions of integrity are here not extravagant. As, under our institutions, public men will be, upon the whole, fair exponents of the character of their constituents, the plainest way to secure honest public men, is to inspire those who make them, with a right understanding of what political character ought to be. Young men should be prompted to discriminate between the specious — and the real; the artful — and the honest; the wise — and the cunning; the patriotic — and the pretender. I will sketch —

VI. The Demagogue is a political leader who seeks support by appealing to popular desires and prejudices. The lowest of politicians, is that man who seeks to gratify an invariable selfishness — by pretending to seek the public good. For a profitable popularity, he accommodates himself to all opinions, to all dispositions, to every side, and to each prejudice. He is a mirror, with no face of its own — but a smooth surface from which each man of ten thousand may see himself reflected. He glides from man to man coinciding with their views, pretending their feelings, simulating their tastes. With this person, he hates a man; with that person, he loves the same man. He favors a law — and he dislikes it. He approves — and opposes. He is on both sides at once. He attends meetings to suppress intemperance — but at elections makes every tavern free to all drinkers. He can with equal relish plead most eloquently for temperance — or drink up a dozen glasses in a dirty tavern.

He thinks that there is a time for everything, and therefore, at one time he swears and jeers and leers with a carousing crew; and at another time, having happily been converted, he displays the various features of devotion. Indeed, he is a capacious Christian — an epitome of faith. He was always a Methodist and always shall be — until he meets a Presbyterian; then he is a Presbyterian, old-school or new, as the case requires. However, as he is not a bigot

— he can afford to be a Baptist, in a good Baptist neighborhood, and with a wink he tells the zealous elder, that he never had one of his children baptized, not he! He whispers to the Reformer that he abhors all creeds but the Bible. After all this, room will be found in his heart for the fugitive sects also, which come and go like clouds in a summer sky. His flattering attention at church edifies the simple-hearted preacher, who admires that a plain sermon should make a man whisper amen! and weep.

Upon the platform, his tact is no less rare. He roars and bawls with courageous plainness, on points about which all agree: but on subjects where men differ, his meaning is nicely balanced on a pivot that it may dip either way. He depends for success chiefly upon humorous stories. A glowing patriot telling stories is a dangerous antagonist; for it is hard to expose the fallacy of a hearty laugh, and men convulsed with merriment are slow to perceive in what way an argument is a reply to a story.

Perseverance, effrontery, good nature, and versatile cunning — have advanced many a bad man higher than a good man could attain. Men will admit that he has not a single moral virtue — but he is smart. We object to no man for amusing himself at the fertile resources of the politician here painted; for sober men are sometimes pleased with the grimaces and mischievous tricks of a versatile monkey; but would it not be strange indeed if they should select him for a ruler, or make him an exemplar to their sons?

7. The Party Man. I describe next a more respectable and more dangerous politician — the Party Man. He has associated his ambition, his interests, and his affections with a political party. He prefers, doubtless, that his side

should be victorious by the best means, and under the championship of good men; but rather than lose the victory, he will consent to any means, and follow any man. Thus, with a general desire to be upright — the exigency of his party constantly pushes him to dishonorable deeds. He opposes fraud by craft; lie, by lie; slander, by counter-aspersion. To be sure, it is wrong to mis-state, to distort, to suppress or color facts; it is wrong to employ the evil passions; to set class against class; the poor against the rich, the country against the city, the farmer against the mechanic, one section against another section. But his opponents do it, and if they will take advantage of men's corruption — so he must, or lose by his virtue.

He gradually adopts two characters, a personal and a political character. All the requisitions of his conscience, he obeys in his private character; all the requisitions of his party, he obeys in his political conduct. In one character he is a man of principle; in the other, a man of mere expedients. As a man, he means to be genuine, honest, moral; as a politician, he is deceitful, cunning, unscrupulous — anything for party. As a man, he abhors the slimy demagogue; as a politician, he employs him as a scavenger. As a man, he shrinks from the flagitiousness of slander; as a politician, he permits it, smiles upon it in others, rejoices in the success gained by it. As a man, he respects no one who is rotten in heart; as a politician, no man through whom victory may be gained can be too bad. As a citizen, he is an apostle of temperance; as a politician, he puts his shoulder under the men who deluge their track with whisky, marching a crew of brawling patriots, pugnaciously drunk, to exercise the freeman's noblest franchise — the Vote. As a citizen, he is considerate of the young, and counsels them with admirable wisdom; then, as a politician, he votes for aspirants scraped from the ditch, the tavern, and the brothel; thus saying by deeds which the young are quick to understand: "I jested, when I warned you of bad company; for you perceive none worse than those whom I delight to honor."

For his religion, he will give up all his secular interests; but for his politics, he gives up even his religion. He adores virtue — and rewards vice. While bolstering up unrighteous measures, and more unrighteous men — he prays for the advancement of religion, and justice, and honor! I would to God that his prayer might be answered upon his own political head; for never was there a place where such blessings were more needed!

I am puzzled to know what will happen at death to this political Christian — but most unchristian politician. Will both of his characters go heavenward together? If the strongest prevails — he will certainly go to Hell. If his weakest, (which is his Christian character,) is saved — then what will become of his political character? Shall he be sawn in two, as Solomon proposed to divide the contested infant? If this style of character were not flagitiously wicked, it would still be supremely ridiculous — but it is both! Let young men mark these amphibious exemplars, to avoid their influence. The young have nothing to gain from those who are saints in religion and morals, and devils in politics; who have partitioned off their heart, invited Christ into one half, and Belial into the other.

It is wisely said, that a strictly honest man who desires purely the public good, who will not criminally flatter the people, nor take part in lies, or party-slander, nor descend to the arts of the rat, the weasel, and the fox — cannot succeed in politics. It is calmly said by thousands that one cannot be a politician — and a Christian. Indeed, a man is liable to downright ridicule, if he speaks in good earnest of a scrupulously honest and religiously moral politician. I regard all such representations as false. We are not without men whose career is a refutation of the slander. It poisons the community to teach this fatal necessity of corruption, in a course which so many must pursue. It is not strange, if such be the popular opinion, that young men include the sacrifice of strict integrity, as a necessary element of a political life, and calmly agree to it, as to an inevitable misfortune, rather than to a dark and voluntary crime!

Only if a man is an ignorant heathen, can he escape blame for such a decision! A young man, at this day, in this land, who can coolly purpose a life of most unmanly deceit, who means to earn his bread and fame by a sacrifice of integrity — is one who requires only temptation and opportunity to become a felon!

What a heart has that man, who can stand in the very middle of the Bible, with its transcendent truths raising their glowing fronts on every side of him, and feel no inspiration, but that of immorality and baseness! He knows that for him have been founded the perpetual institutions of religion; for him prophets have spoken, miracles been wrought, Heaven robbed of its Magistrate, and the earth made sacred above all planets as the Redeemer's birth and death place — he knows it all, and plunges from this height to the very bottom of corruption! He hears that he is immortal, and despises the immortality; that he is a creation of God, and scorns the dignity; a potential heir of Heaven, and infamously sells his heirship, and himself, for a contemptible mess of loathsome pottage!

Do not tell me of any excuses. It is a shame to attempt an excuse! If there were no religion, if that vast sphere, out of which glow all the supereminent truths of the Bible, was a mere emptiness and void — yet, methinks, the very idea of Fatherland, the exceeding preciousness of the Laws and Liberties of a great people — would enkindle such a high and noble enthusiasm, that all baser feelings would be consumed! But if . . .

>the love of country,
>a sense of character,
>a manly regard for integrity,
>the example of our most illustrious men,
>the warnings of religion and all its solicitations,
>and the prospect of the future — as dark as Perdition

to the evil, and as bright as Paradise to the holy
— cannot inspire a young man to anything higher than a sneaking, truckling, dodging scramble for fraudulent fame and dishonest bread — it is because such a creature has never felt one sensation of manly virtue — it is because his heart is a howling wilderness, inhospitable to innocence!

Thus have I sketched a few of the characters which abound in every community; dangerous, not more by their direct temptations, than by their insensible influence. The sight of their deeds, of their temporary success, their apparent happiness . . .

>relaxes the tense rigidity of a scrupulous honesty,
>inspires a ruinous liberality of sentiment toward vice,
>and breeds the thoughts of evil. And Evil Thoughts are

the cockatrice's eggs, hatching into all Evil Deeds.

Remember, if by any of these you are enticed to ruin, you will have to bear it alone! They are strong to seduce — but heartless to sustain their victims. They will . . .

>exhaust your means,

teach you to despise the God of your fathers,
lead you into every sin,

go with you while you afford them any pleasure or profit — and then, when the inevitable disaster of wickedness begins to overwhelm you — they will abandon whom they have debauched!

When, at length, DEATH gnaws at your bones and knocks at your heart; when staggering, and worn out, your courage wasted, your hope gone, your purity gone, and long, long ago your peace gone — will he who first enticed your steps, now serve your extremity with one office of kindness? Will he encourage you? — cheer your dying agony with one word of hope? — or light the way for your coward steps to the grave? — or weep when you are gone? — or send one pitiful scrap to your desolate family? What reveler wears death-crape for a dead drunkard? — what gang of gamblers ever intermitted a game for the death of a companion? — or went on kind missions of relief to broken-down fellow-gamblers? What harlot weeps for a harlot? — what debauchee mourns for a debauchee? They would carouse at your funeral — and gamble on your coffin! If one flush more of pleasure were to be had by it, they would drink shame and ridicule to your memory out of your own skull — and roar in bacchanalian-revelry over your damnation!

All the shameless atrocities of wicked men, are nothing to their heartlessness toward each other when broken-down. As I have seen worms writhing on a carcass, crawling over each other, and elevating their fiery heads in petty ferocity against each other, while all were enshrined in the corruption of a common carrion — I have thought, ah! shameful picture of wicked men tempting each other, abetting each other, until calamity overtook them — and then fighting and devouring or abandoning each other, without pity, or sorrow, or compassion, or remorse!

Evil men of every degree will use you, flatter you, lead you on until you are useless; then, if the virtuous do not pity you, or God compassionate you — you are without a friend in the universe!

"My son, if sinners entice you — do not give in to them. If they say: 'Come along with us; let's lie in wait for someone's blood, let's waylay some harmless soul; let's swallow them alive, like the grave, and whole, like those who go down to the pit! We will get all sorts of valuable things and fill our houses with plunder; throw in your lot with us, and we will share a common purse.' My son, do not go along with them, do not set foot on their paths; for their feet rush into sin, they are swift to shed blood. These men lie in wait for their own blood; they waylay only themselves!" Proverbs 1:10-18

Popular Amusements

Henry Ward Beecher, 1849

I am to venture the delicate task of reprehension, always unwelcome, but peculiarly offensive upon topics of popular amusement. I am anxious, in the beginning, to put myself right with the young. If I satisfy myself, Christian men, and the sober community, and do not satisfy the young people — then my success will be like a physician's, whose prescriptions please himself, but do good to everybody except the patient — he dies.

Allow me, first of all, to satisfy you that I am not meddling with matters which do not concern me. When we speak a word against sinful amusements, we are met with the surly answer, "Why do you meddle with things which don't concern you? If you do not enjoy these pleasures, why do you discourage those who do? May not men do as they please in a free country, without being hung up in a gibbet of public remark?"

It is conveniently forgotten, I suppose, that in a free country we have the same right to criticize sinful amusements, which others have to enjoy it. Indeed, you and I both know, young gentlemen, that in ale-house circles, and in nocturnal convivial feasts, the Church is regarded as little better than a spectacled old bedlam, whose impertinent eyes are spying everybody's business but her own; and who, too old or too homely to be tempted herself, with compulsory virtue, pouts at the joyous dalliances of the young and mirthful. Religion is called a nun, sable with gloomy vestments; and the Church a cloister, where ignorance is deemed innocence, and which sends out querulous reprehensions of a world, which it knows nothing about, and has professedly abandoned. This is pretty; and is only defective, in not being true. The Church is not a cloister, nor her members recluses, nor are our censures of vice intermeddling. Not to dwell in generalities, let us take a plain and common case:

A company offer to educate our youth; and to show the community the road of morality, which, probably they have not seen themselves for twenty years. We cannot help laughing at a generosity so much above one's means: and when they proceed to hew and hack each other with rusty iron, to teach our boys valor; and dress up charlatans, to teach theoretical virtue; if we laugh somewhat more, they turn upon us testily: "Mind your own business, and leave us with ours. We do not interfere with your preaching."

But may not Christian people amuse themselves with very diverting men from destruction? I hope it is not bigotry to have eyes and ears: I hope it is not fanaticism, in the use of these excellent senses, for us to judge that throwing one's heels higher than their head a-dancing, is not exactly the way to teach virtue to our daughters; and that unchaste women, are not the people to teach virtue, at any rate. Oh! no; we are told, Christians must not know that all this is very singular. Christians ought to think that men who are actors on the stage, are virtuous men, even if they gamble at night, and are drunk all day; and if men are so used to comedy, that their life becomes a perpetual farce on morality, we have no right to laugh at this extra professional acting!

Are we meddlers, who only seek the good of our own families, and of our own community where we live and expect to die?

I am anxious to put all Christian men in their right position before you; and in this controversy between them and the mirthful world, to show you the facts upon both sides. A floating population, in pairs or companies, without permission asked — blow the trumpet for all our youth to flock to their banners! Are they related to them? — are they concerned in the welfare of our town? — do they live among us? — do they bear any part of our burdens? — do they care for our substantial citizens? We grade our streets, build our schools, support all our municipal laws, and the young men are ours; our sons, our brothers, our wards, clerks, or apprentices; they are living in our houses, work in our stores and our shops, and we are their guardians, and take care of them in health, and watch them in sickness. Yet every vagabond who floats in hither, swears and swaggers, as if they were all his: and when they offer to corrupt all these youth, we paying them round sums of money for it, and we get courage finally to say that we had rather not; that industry and honesty are better than expert knavery — they turn upon us in great indignation with, "Why don't you mind your own business — what are you meddling with our affairs for?"

I will suppose a case. With much painstaking, I have saved enough money to buy a little garden-spot. I put all around it a good fence — I put the spade into it and mellow the soil full deep; I go to the nursery and pick out choice fruit trees — I select the best seeds of the rarest vegetables; and so my garden thrives. I know every inch of it, for I have watered every inch with sweat.

One morning I am awakened by a mixed sound of sawing, digging, and delving; and looking out, I see a dozen men at work in my garden. I run down and find one man sawing out a huge hole in the fence. "My dear sir, what are you doing?" "Oh, this high fence is very troublesome to climb over; I am fixing an easier way for folks to get in."

Another man has cut branches off several choice trees, and is putting in new grafts. "Sir, what are you changing the kind for?" "Oh, this kind don't suit me; I like a new kind."

One man is digging up my beans, to plant cockles; another is rooting up my strawberries, to put in parsley; and another is destroying my blueberries, and gooseberries, and raspberries, to plant mustard and weeds. At last, I lose all patience, and cry out, "Well, gentlemen, this will never do. I will never tolerate this abominable imposition; you are ruining my garden." One of them says, "You old hypocritical bigot! mind your business, and let us enjoy ourselves. Take care of your house, and do not pry into cur pleasures."

Fellow-citizens! I own that no man could so invade your garden; but men are allowed thus to invade our town, and destroy our children! You will let them evade your laws, to fleece and demoralize you; and you sit down under their railing, as though you were the intruders! — just as if the man, who drives a thief out of his house, ought to ask the rascal's pardon for interfering with his little plans of pleasure and profit!

Every parent has a right — every citizen and every minister has the same right, to expose evil traps, which men have set; the same right to prevent mischief, which men have plotted; the same right to attack vice, which vice has to attack virtue; a better right to save our sons and brothers, and companions, than artful men have to destroy them.

The necessity of amusement, is admitted on all hands. There is an appetite of the eye, of the ear, and of every sense, for which God has provided the material. Gaiety of every degree, this side of puerile levity, is wholesome to the body, to the mind, and to the morals.

Nature is a vast repository of manly enjoyments. The magnitude of God's works is not less admirable than its exhilarating beauty. The crudest forms have something of beauty; the ruggedest strength is graced with some charm; the very pins, and rivets, and clasps of nature, are attractive by qualities of beauty more than is necessary for mere utility. The sun could go down without gorgeous clouds; evening could advance without its evanescent brilliance; trees might have flourished without symmetry; flowers have existed without fragrance, and fruit without flavor.

When I have journeyed through forests, where ten thousand shrubs and vines exist without apparent use; through prairies, whose undulations exhibit sheets of flowers innumerable, and absolutely dazzling the eye with their prodigality of beauty — beauty, not a fraction of which is ever seen by man — it is plain that God is himself passionately fond of beauty, and the earth is his garden, as an acre is man's.

God has made us like Himself, to be pleased by the universal beauty of the world. He has made provision in nature, in society, and in the family — for amusement and exhilaration enough to fill the heart with the perpetual sunshine of delight.

Upon this broad earth, purpled with flowers, scented with fragrances, brilliant in colors, vocal with echoing and re-echoing melody — I take my stand against all demoralizing pleasures. Is it not enough that our Father's house is so full of dear delights, that we must wander prodigal to the swine-herd for husks, and to the slough for drink? — when the trees of God's heritage bend over our head, and solicit our hand to pluck the golden fruitage, must we still go in search of the apples of Sodom — outside fair, and inside ashes?

Men shall crowd to the Circus to hear clowns, and see rare feats of horsemanship; but a bird may poise beneath the very sun, or flying downward, swoop from the high Heaven; then flit with graceful ease hither and there, pouring liquid song as if it were a perennial fountain of sound — no man cares for that.

Upon the stage of life, the vastest tragedies are performing in every act; nations pitching headlong to their final catastrophe; others, raising their youthful forms to begin the drama of their existence.

The world of society is as full of exciting interest, as nature is full of beauty. The great dramatic throng of life is hustling along — the wise, the fool, the clown, the miser, the bereaved, the broken-hearted. Life mingles before us smiles and tears, sighs and laughter, joy and gloom — as the spring mingles the winter-storm and summer-sunshine.

To this vast Theater which God has built, where stranger plays are seen than ever any author wrote — man seldom cares to come. When God dramatizes, when nations act, or all the human kind conspire to educe the vast catastrophe — men sleep and snore, and let the busy scene go on, unlooked, unthought upon; and turn from all its varied magnificence to hunt out some candle-lighted hole and gaze at drunken ranters, or cry at the piteous virtue of harlots in distress.

It is my object then, not to withdraw the young from pleasure, but from unworthy pleasures; not to lessen their enjoyments, but to increase them by rejecting the counterfeit and the vile.

Of gambling, I have already sufficiently spoken. Of cock-fighting, dog-fighting, and pugilistic contests, I need to speak but little. These are the desperate excitements of debauched men; but no man becomes desperately criminal, until he has been genteelly criminal. No one spreads his sail upon such waters, at first; these brutal amusements are but the gulf into which flow all the streams of criminal pleasures; and they who embark upon the river, are sailing toward the gulf. Wretches who have waded all the depths of iniquity, and burned every passion to the socket, find in rage and blows and blood — the only stimulus of which they are susceptible. You are training yourselves to be just such wretches, if you are exhausting your passions in such illicit indulgences.

As it is impossible to analyze, separately, each wicked amusement offered to the young, I am compelled to select two, each the representative of a clan. Thus, the reasonings applied to the amusement of Racing, apply equally well to all violent amusements which congregate indolent and dissipated men, by ministering intense excitement. The reasonings applied to the Theater, with some modifications, apply to the Circus, to promiscuous balls, to night-reveling, bacchanalian feasts, and to other similar indulgences.

Many, who are not in danger, may incline to turn from these pages; they live in rural districts, in villages, or towns, and are out of the reach of fighters, and actors, and gamblers. This is the very reason why you should read.

We are such a migratory, restless people, that our home is usually everywhere but at home; and almost every young man makes annual, or biennial visits to famous cities; conveying produce to market, or purchasing wares and goods. It is at such times that the young are in extreme danger; for they are particularly anxious, at such times, to appear at their full age. A young man is ashamed, in a great hotel, to seem raw and not to know the mysteries of the bar and of the town. They put on a very remarkable air, which is meant for ease; they affect profusion of expense; they think it fit for a gentleman to know all that certain other city gentlemen seem proud of knowing.

As sober citizens are not found lounging at taverns; and the gentlemanly part of the traveling community are usually retiring, modest, and unnoticeable — the young are left to come in contact chiefly with a very flashy class of men who swarm about city restaurateurs and taverns — drunken clerks, crack sportsmen, epicures, and rich, green youth, seasoning. These are the most numerous class which engage the attention of the young. They bustle in the sitting room, or crowd the bar, assume the chief seats at the table, and play the petty lord in a manner so brilliant, as altogether to dazzle our poor country boy, who mourns at his deficient education, at the poverty of his rural entertainments, and the meagerness of those illicit pleasures, which he formerly nibbled at with mouselike stealth; and he sighs for these riper entertainments.

Besides, it is well known, that large commercial establishments have, residing at such hotels, well appointed clerks to draw customers to their counter. It is their business to make your acquaintance, to fish out the probable condition of your funds, to sweeten your temper with delicate tit-bits of pleasure; to take you to the Theater, and a little further on, if need be; to draw you in to a generous supper, and initiate you to the high life of men whose whole life is only the varied phases of lust, gastronomical or amorous.

Besides these, there lurk in such places lynx-eyed procurers; men who have an interest in your appetites; who look upon a young man, with some money, just as a butcher looks upon a bullock — a thing of so many pounds fatness, of so much beef, so much tallow, and a hide. If you have nothing, they will have nothing to do with you; if you have means, they undertake to supply you with the disposition to use them. They know the city, they know its haunts, they know its secret doors, its blind passages, its spicy pleasures, its racy vices, clear down to the mud-slime of the very bottom!

Meanwhile, the accustomed restraint of home cast off, the youth feels that he is unknown, and may do what he chooses, unexposed. There is, moreover, an intense curiosity to see many things of which he has long ago heard and wondered; and it is the very art and education of vice, to make itself attractive. It comes with garlands of roses about its brow, with nectar in its goblet, and love upon its tongue.

If you have, beforehand, no settled opinions as to what is right and what is wrong; if your judgment, for the first time, is to be formed upon the propriety of your actions; if you are not controlled by settled moral principles — there is scarcely a chance for your purity!

For this purpose, then, I desire to discuss these things, that you may settle your opinions and principles before temptation assails you. As a ship is built upon the dry shore, which afterwards is to dare the storm and brave the sea — so would I build you staunch and strong, before you be launched abroad upon life!

I. Horse Racing. This amusement justifies its existence by the plea of Utility. We will examine it upon its own ground. Who are the patrons of the race-course? — farmers? — laborers? — men who are practically the most interested in the improvement of livestock? The unerring instinct of self-interest would lead these men to patronize the race-course, if its utility were real. It is notorious that these are not the patrons of racing.

It is sustained by two classes of men — gambling jockeys and jaded rich men. In England, and in our own country, where the races are freshest, they owe their existence entirely to the extraordinary excitement which they afford to dissipation, or to cloyed appetites. For those industrial purposes for which the horse is chiefly valuable, for transportation and work, what do the patrons of the race-care? Their whole anxiety is centered upon winning and stakes; and that is incomparably the best horse which will run the longest space in the shortest time. The points required for this are not, and never will be, the points for substantial service.

And it is notorious, that racing in England has deteriorated the horse stock in such important respects, that the cavalry and police service suffered severely. New England, where racing is almost unknown, is to this day the place where the horse exists in the finest qualities; and for all economical purposes, Virginia and Kentucky must yield to New England. Except for the sole purpose of racing, an Eastern horse brings a higher price than any other.

The other class of patrons who sustain a race-course are mere gambling jockeys. As crows to a corn-field, or vultures to their prey; as flies to summer-sweet — so to the annual races, flow the whole tribe of gamblers and pleasure-lovers. It is the Jerusalem of wicked men; and there the tribes go up, like Israel of old, but for a far different sacrifice.

No form of social abomination is unknown or unpracticed; and if all the good that is claimed, and a hundred times more, were done to horses, it would be a dear bargain. To ruin men for the sake of improving horses; to sacrifice conscience and purity for the sake of good bones and muscles in a beast — this is paying a little too much for good brutes. Indeed, the shameless immorality, the perpetual and growing dishonesty, the almost immeasurable secret villainy of the horse race, has alarmed and disgusted many stalwart racers, who, having no objection to some evil, are appalled at the very ocean of depravity which rolls before them. I extract the words of one of the leading sportsmen of England: "How many fine domains have been shared among these hosts of rapacious sharks, during the last two hundred years; and, unless the system is altered, how many more are doomed to fall into the same gulf! For, we lament to say, the evil has increased: all heretofore has been 'Tarts And Cheese-Cakes' compared to the villainous proceedings of the last twenty years at the English races."

I will drop this barbarous amusement, with a few questions.

What have you, young men, to do with the race-course, admitting it to be what it claims, a school for horses? Are you particularly interested in that branch of learning?

Is it safe to accustom yourselves to such tremendous excitement as that of racing?

Is the invariable company of such places of a kind which you ought to be found in? — will races make you more moral? — more industrious? — more careful? — more economical? — more trustworthy?

You who have attended them, what advice would you give a young man, a younger brother for instance, who should seriously ask if he had better attend?

I digress to say one word to women. When a race-course was opened at Cincinnati, ladies would not attend it; when one was opened here, ladies would not attend it — and for very good reasons — they were Ladies. If it be said that they attend the Races in the South and in England, I reply, that they do a great many other things which you would not choose to do.

Roman ladies could see hundreds of gladiators stab and hack each other — could you? Spanish ladies can see savage bull-fights — would you? It is possible for a modest woman to countenance very questionable practices, where the customs of society and the universal public opinion approve them. But no woman can set herself against public opinion, in favor of an immoral sport, without being herself immoral; for, if worse be wanting, it is immorality enough for a woman to put herself where her reputation will lose its suspiciousless luster.

II. The Theater.

Desperate efforts are made, year by year, to increase this corrupting evil. Its claims are put forth with vehemence. Let us examine them.

1. They claim that the theater cultivates the taste. Let the appeal be to facts. Let the roll of English literature be explored — our Poets, Romancers, Historians, Essayists, Critics, and Divines — and for what part of their memorable writings are we indebted to the theater? If we except one period of our literature, the claim is wholly groundless; and at this day, the truth is so opposite to the claim, that extravagance, affectation, and rant, are proverbially denominated theatrical.

If agriculture should attempt to supersede the admirable implements of husbandry, now in use, by the primitive plough or sharpened sticks — it would not be more absurd than to advocate that clumsy machine of literature, the Theater — by the side of the popular lecture, the pulpit, and the press. It is not congenial to our age or necessities. Its day is gone by — it is in its senility, as might be suspected, from the weakness of the garrulous apologies which it puts forth.

2. They claim that the theater is a school of morals. Yes, doubtless! So the guillotine is defended on the plea of humanity. Inquisitors declare their racks and torture-beds to be the instruments of love, affectionately admonishing the fallen of the error of their ways. The slave-trade has been defended on the plea of humanity, and slavery is now defended for its mercies. Were it necessary for any school

or party, doubtless we should hear arguments to prove the Devil's grace, and the utility of his agency among men.

But, let me settle these impudent pretensions to Theater-virtue, by the home thrust of a few plain questions.

Will any of you who have been to Theaters, please to tell me whether virtue ever received important accessions from the gallery of Theaters?

Will you tell me whether the Theater is a place where an ordinarily virtuous man would love to seat his children?

Was ever a Theater known where a prayer at the opening, and a prayer at the close, would not be tormentingly discordant?

How does it happen, that in a school for morals — the teachers never learn their own lessons?

Would you allow a son or daughter to associate alone with actors or actresses?

Do these men who promote virtue so zealously when acting, take any part in public moral enterprises, when their stage dresses are off?

Which would surprise you most, to see actors steadily at Church, or to see Christians steadily at a Theater? Would not both strike you as singular incongruities?

What is the reason that loose and abandoned men abhor religion in a Church — and love it so much in a Theater?

Since the Theater is the handmaid of virtue, why are drinking houses so necessary to its neighborhood, yet so offensive to Churches? The trustees of the Tremont Theater in Boston, publicly protested against an order of council forbidding liquor to be sold on the premises, on the ground that it was impossible to support the Theater without it.

3. I am told that Christians attend the Theaters. Then I will tell them the story of the Ancients. A holy monk reproached the devil for stealing a young man who was found at the Theater. He promptly replied, "I found him on my premises, and took him."

But, it is said, if Christians would take Theaters in hand, instead of abandoning them to loose men — they might become the handmaids of religion.

The Church has had an intimate acquaintance with the Theater for eighteen hundred years. During that period, every available agent for the diffusion of morality into it has been earnestly tried. The result is, that familiarity has bred contempt and abhorrence. If, after so long and thorough an acquaintance, the Church stands the mortal enemy of Theaters, the testimony is conclusive. It is the evidence of generations speaking by the most sober, thinking, and honest men.

Let not this vagabond prostitute pollute any longer the precincts of the Church, with impudent proposals of alliance. When the Church needs an alliance, it will not look for it in the kennel. Ah! what a blissful scene would that be — the Church and Theater imparadised in each other's arms! What a sweet conjunction would be made, could we build our Churches so as to preach in the morning, and play in the theaters by night! And how melting it would be, beyond the love of David and Jonathan, to see minister and actor in loving embrace; one slaying Satan by direct thrusts of plain preaching — and the other sucking his very life out by the enchantment of the Drama!

To this millennial scene of Church and Theater, I only suggest a single improvement: that the church building be enlarged to a ring for a Circus, when not needed for prayer-meetings; that the Sabbath-school room should be furnished with dice and card-tables, and useful texts of scripture might be printed on the cards, for the pious meditations of gamblers during the intervals of play and worship.

4. But if theaters are put down, men will go to worse vices. Where will they find worse ones? Are those who go to the Theater, the Circus, the Race-course, the men who abstain from worse places? It is notorious that the crowd of theater-goers are vomited up from these worse places. It is notorious that the Theater is the door to all the sinks of iniquity. It is through this infamous place that the young learn to love those wicked associates and practices to which, else, they would have been strangers. Half the victims of the gallows and of the Penitentiary will tell you, that these schools for morals were to them the gate of debauchery, the porch of pollution, the vestibule of the very house of Death!

5. The theater makes one acquainted with human life, and with human nature. It is too true. There is scarcely an evil incident to human life, which may not be fully learned at the Theater. Here flourishes every variety of wit —

ridicule of sacred things, burlesques of religion, and licentious double-entendres. Nowhere can so much of this lore be learned, in so short a time, as at the Theater! There one learns how pleasant a thing is vice; immorality prospers; and the young come away alive to the glorious liberty of conquest and lust.

But the stage is not the only place about the Drama where human nature is learned. In the Boxes the young may make the acquaintance of those who abhor home and domestic quiet; of those who glory in profusion and obtrusive display; of those who expend all, and more than their earnings, upon mirthful clothes and jewelry; of those who think it no harm to borrow their money without permission from their employer's til; of those who despise vulgar appetite, but affect polished and genteel licentiousness.

Or, he may go to the Theater, and learn the whole round of villain-life from masters in the art. He may sit down among thieves, blood-loving scoundrels, swindlers, broken-down men of pleasure — the coarse, the vulgar, the debauched, the inhuman, the infernal.

Or, if still more of human nature is wished, he can learn yet more; for the Theater epitomizes every degree of corruption. Let the virtuous young scholar go to the Theater, and learn there, decency, modesty, and refinement, among the quarreling, drunken, ogling, mincing, brutal women of the brothel!

Ah! there is no place like the Theater for learning human nature! A young man can gather up more experimental knowledge here in a week, than elsewhere in a year.

But I wonder that the Theater should ever confess the fact; and yet more, that it should lustily plead in self-defense, that Theaters teach men so much of human nature! Here are brilliant bars, to teach the young to drink; here are mirthful companions, to undo in half an hour, the scruples formed by an education of years; here are pimps of pleasure, to delude the brain with bewildering sophisms of immorality; here is pleasure, all flushed in its gayest, boldest, most fascinating forms! Few there be who can resist its wiles, and fewer yet who can yield to them and escape ruin.

If you would pervert the taste — then go to the Theater.

If you would imbibe false views of life — then go to the Theater.

If you would efface as speedily as possible all qualms of conscience — then go to the Theater.

If you would put yourself irreconcilably against the spirit of virtue and religion — then go to the Theater.

If you would be infected with each particular vice in the catalogue of Depravity — then go to the Theater.

Let parents, who wish to make their children weary of home and quiet domestic enjoyments — take them to the Theater. If it be desirable for the young to loathe industry and education, and burn for fierce excitements, and seek them by stealth or through pilferings, if need be — then send them to the Theater!

It is notorious that the bill of fare at these temples of pleasure is made up to the taste of the baser appetites; that base comedy, and baser farce, running into absolute obscenity — are the only means of filling a house. Theaters must be corrupt, to live; and those who attend them will be corrupted!

Let me turn your attention to several reasons which should incline every young man to forswear such immoral amusements.

1. The first reason is, their waste of TIME. I do not mean that they waste only the time consumed while you are within them; but they make you waste your time afterwards. You will go once — and wish to go again; you will go twice, and seek it a third time; you will go a third time — a fourth; and whenever the Theater opens, you will be seized with a restlessness and craving to go, until the appetite will become a passion. You will then waste your nights: your mornings being heavy, melancholy, and dull — you will waste them. Your day will next be confused and crowded; your duties poorly executed or deferred; habits of arrant slothfulness will ensue; and day by day, industry will grow tiresome, and leisure sweeter, until you are a waster of time — an idle man; and if not a rogue, you will be a fortunate exception.

2. You ought not to countenance these things because they will waste your MONEY. Young gentlemen! Wasting and squandering is as shameful as hoarding. A fool can throw away — and a fool can lock up; but it is a wise man, who, neither stingy nor profuse, steers the middle course of

generous economy and frugal liberality. A young man, at first, thinks that all he spends at such places, is the ticket-price of the Theater, or the small bet on the races; and this he knows is not much. But this is certainly not the whole bill — nor half.

First, you pay your entrance fee. But there are a thousand petty luxuries which one must not neglect, or custom will call him niggard. You must buy your cigars, and your friend's. You must buy your juleps, and treat in your turn. You must occasionally wait on your lady, and she must be comforted with divers confections. You cannot go to such places in homely working dress — new and costlier clothes must be bought. All your companions have jewelry — you will need a ring, or a gold watch, or an ebony cane, or some other luxury. Thus, item presses upon item, and in the year a long bill runs up of money spent for little trifles.

But if all this money could buy you off from the yet worse effects, the bargain would not be so dear. But compare, if you please, this mode of expenditure with the principle of your ordinary expense. In all ordinary and business-transactions you get an equivalent for your money — either food for nourishment, or clothes for comfort, or permanent property. But when a young man has spent one or two hundred dollars for the Theater, Circus, Races, Balls, and reveling — what has he to show for it at the end of the year? Nothing at all good — and much that is bad! You sink your money as really as if you threw it into the sea; and you do it in such a way that you form habits of careless expense. You lose all sense of the value of property; and when a man sees no value in property, he will see no necessity for labor; and when he is both lazy and careless of property, he will become dishonest. Thus, a habit which seems innocent — the habit of trifling with money — often degenerates to slothfulness, indolence, and roguery.

3. Such pleasures are incompatible with your ordinary pursuits. The very way to ruin an honest business is to be ashamed of it, or to put alongside of it, something which a man loves better. There can be no industrial calling so exciting as the Theater, the Circus, and the Races. If you wish to make your real employment very dull and hateful, visit such places. After the glare of the Theater has dazzled your eyes — your blacksmith-shop will look smuttier than ever it did before. After you have seen stalwart heroes pounding their antagonists — you will find it a dull business to pound iron. And a faithful apprentice who has seen such gracious glances of love and such rapturous kissing of hands — will hate to dirty his heroic fingers with mortar, or by rolling felt on the hatter's board.

If a man had a plain, but most useful wife — patient, kind, intelligent, hopeful in sorrow, and cheerful in prosperity, but yet very plain — would he be wise to bring under his roof a fascinating and seductive beauty? Would the contrast, and her fascinations, make him love his own wife better? Young gentlemen, your wives are your industrial calling! These theater beauties are artful jades, dressed up on purpose to purloin your affections. Let no man be led to commit adultery with a Theater, against the rights of his own trade.

4. Another reason why you should let alone these deceitful pleasures is, that they will engage you in BAD COMPANY. To the Theater, the Ball, the Circus, the Race-

course, the gambling-table — resort all the idle, the dissipated, the rogues, the licentious, the epicures, the gluttons, the artful jades, the immoral, the worthless, the refuse. When you go, you will not, at first, take introduction to them all, but to those nearest like yourself; by them the way will be open to others.

A very great evil has befallen a young virtuous man, when wicked men feel that they have a right to his acquaintance. When I see a gambler slapping a young mechanic on the back; or a lecherous scoundrel suffusing a young man's cheek by a story at which, despite his blushes, he yet laughs — I know the youth has been guilty of criminal indiscretion, or these men could not approach him thus. That is a brave and strong heart that can stand up pure in a company of seductive wretches.

When wicked men mean to seduce a young man, so tremendous are the odds in favor of practiced experience against innocence, that there is not one chance in a thousand — if the young man lets them approach him. Let every young man remember that he carries, by nature, a heart full of passions, just such as bad men have. With youth these passions slumber; but temptation can wake them, bad men can influence them — they know the road, they know how to serenade the heart; how to raise the sash, and elope with each passion.

There is but one resource for innocence among men or women; and that is, an embargo upon all commerce of bad men. Bar the window! — bolt the door! — nor answer their seductions, even if they charm ever so wisely! In no other way can you be safe. So well am I assured of the power of bad men to seduce the erring purity of man, that I pronounce it next to impossible for man or woman to escape, if they permit bad men to approach and dally with them.

Oh! there is more than magic in temptation, when it beams down upon the heart of man, like the sun upon a morass! At the noontide-hour of purity, the mists shall rise and wreathe a thousand fantastic forms of delusion; and a sudden outbreak of passion, a single gleam of the imagination, one sudden rush of the capricious heart — and the resistance of years may be prostrated in a moment, the heart entered by the besieging enemy, its rooms sought out, and every lovely affection rudely seized by the invader's lust, and given to ravishment and to ruin!

5. Putting together in one class, all gamblers, circus-people, actors and racing-jockeys — I pronounce them to be men who live off of society without returning any useful equivalent. At the most lenient sentence, they are a band of mirthful idlers. They do not throw one cent into the stock of public good. They do not make shoes, or hats, or houses, or harness, or anything else that is useful. A stableboy is useful; he performs a necessary office. A street-sweeper, a chimney-sweep, the seller of old clothes, a tinker — all these men are respectable; for though their callings are very humble, they are founded on the real needs of society. The bread which such men eat, is the representation of what they have done for society; not the bread of idleness, but of usefulness.

But what do pleasure-mongers do for a living? — what useful service do they do? — what do they make? — what do they repair? — what do they for the mind, for the body, for man, or child, or beast? The dog that gnaws a refuse bone, pays for it in barking at a thief. The cat that purrs its gratitude for a morsel of meat, will clear our house of rats. But what do we get in return for supporting whole loads of play-actors, and circus-clowns? They eat, they drink, they giggle, they grimace, they strut in garish clothes — and what else? They have not afforded even useful amusement; they are professional laugh-makers; their trade is comic or tragic buffoonery — the trade of tickling men. We do not feel any need of them, before they come; and when they leave, the only effects resulting from their visits are, unruly boys, aping apprentices, and unsteady workmen.

Now, upon principles of mere political economy, is it wise to support a growing class of wasteful idlers? If at the top

of society, the government should erect a class of favored citizens, and pamper their idleness with fat pensions — the indignation of the whole community would break out against such privileged aristocrats. But we have, at the bottom of society, a set of wandering, jesting, dancing, fiddling aristocrats, whom we support for the sake of their capers, grins, and caricatures upon life — and no one seems to think this an evil!

6. But even this is cheap, compared with the evil which I shall mention. If these morality-teachers could guarantee us against all evil from their doings, we might pay their support and think it a cheap bargain. But the direct and necessary effect of their pursuit, however, is to debauch and corrupt others!

Those who defend Theaters would scorn to admit actors into their home society. It is within the knowledge of all, that men, who thus cater for public pleasure, are excluded from respectable society. The general fact is not altered by the exceptions — and honorable exceptions there are.

In the support of gamblers, circus-riders, actors, and racing-jockeys, a Christian and industrious people are guilty of supporting mere mischief-makers — men whose very heart is diseased, and whose sores exhale contagion to all around them! We pay moral assassins to stab the purity of our children. We warn our sons of temptation, and yet plant the seeds which shall bristle with all the spikes and thorns of the worst temptation.

If to this strong language, you answer, that these men are generous and jovial, that their very business is to please, that they do not mean to do harm — I reply, that I do not charge them with knowingly trying to produce immorality — but with pursuing a course which produces it, whether they want to or not.

Moral disease, like the plague, is contagious, whether the patient wishes it or not. A vile man infects his children in spite of himself. Criminals make criminals, just as taint makes taint, disease makes disease, and plagues make plagues. Those who run the mirthful round of pleasure cannot help dazzling the young, confounding their industrious habits, and perverting their morals — it is the very nature of their employment.

These debauching and corrupting professions could not be sustained but by the patronage of moral men. Where do the clerks, the apprentices, the dissipated, get their money which buys an entrance? From whom is that money drained, always, in every land, which supports vice?

Unquestionably from the good, the laborious, the careful. The skill, the enterprise, the labor, the good morals of every nation — are always taxed for the expenses of vice. Jails are built out of honest men's earnings. Courts are supported from peaceful men's property. Penitentiaries are built by the toil of virtuous people. Crime never pays its own way. Vice has no hands to work, no head to calculate. Its whole faculty is to corrupt and to waste; and good men, directly or indirectly, foot the bill.

At this time, when we are waiting in vain for the return of that bread which we wastefully cast upon the waters; when, all over the sea, men are fishing up the wrecks of those sunken ships, and full freighted fortunes, which foundered in the sad storm of recent times — some question might be asked about the economy of vice; the economy of paying for our sons' idleness; the economy of maintaining a whole lazy profession of gamblers, racers, actresses, and actors — human, equine and beastly — whose errand is mischief, and luxury, and license, and giggling folly. It ought to be asked of men who groan at a tax, to pay their honest foreign debts — whether they can be taxed to pay the bills of charlatans?

It is astonishing how little the wicked influence of those professions has been considered, which exert themselves mainly to delight the sensual feelings of men. That whole race of men, whose camp is the Theater, the Circus, the Gambling-table, is a race whose instinct is destruction, who live to corrupt, and live off of the corruption which they make. For their support, we sacrifice annual hoards of youthful victims. Even sober Christian men, look smilingly upon the garish outside of these bands of destruction; and while we see the results to be, slothfulness, dissipation, idleness, dishonesty, vice and crime — still they lull us with the lying lyric of "classic drama" and "human life" "morality" "poetry" and "comedy"?

Disguise it as you will, these men of sinful pleasure are, the world over, Corrupters of Youth. Upon no principle of kindness can we tolerate them; no excuse is bold enough; we can take bail from none of their weaknesses — it is not safe to have them abroad even upon excessive bail. You might as well take bail for lions, or allow scorpions to breed in our streets for a suitable license; or raise a tax to fund assassins.

Men whose life is given to evil pleasures are, to ordinary criminals — what a universal pestilence is to a local disease. They fill the air, pervade the community, and bring around every youth an atmosphere of death. Corrupters of youth have no mitigation of their baseness. Their generosity avails nothing, their knowledge nothing, their varied accomplishments nothing. These are only so many facilities for greater evil.

Is a serpent less deadly, because his burnished scales shine? Shall a dove praise and court the vulture, because he has such glossy plumage?

The more talents a bad man has, the more dangerous is he — they are the garlands which cover up the knife with which he will stab. There is no such a thing as good corrupters. You might as well talk of a mild and pleasant murder, a very lenient assassination, or a pious devil. We denounce them; for it is our nature to loathe treacherous corruption.

We mourn over a torn and bleeding lamb — but who mourns the wolf which rent it? We weep for despoiled innocence — but who sheds a tear for the savage fiend who plucks away the flower of virtue?

Even thus, we palliate the sins of generous youth; and their downfall is our sorrow. But for their destroyers, for the corrupters of youth, who practice the infernal chemistry of ruin, and dissolve the young heart in vice — we have neither tears, nor pleas, nor patience. We lift our heart to Him who bears the iron rod of vengeance, and pray for the appointed time of judgment.

You miscreants! You think that you are growing tall, and walking safely, because God has forgotten? The bolt of judgment shall yet smite you! You shall be heard as the falling of an oak in the silent forest — the vaster its growth, the more terrible its resounding downfall!

Oh! you corrupter of youth! I would not have your death, for all the pleasure of your guilty life, a thousand fold. You shall draw near to the shadow of death. To the Christian, these shades are the golden haze which Heaven's light makes, when it meets the earth and mingles with its shadows. But to you, these shall be shadows full of phantom-shapes. Images of terror in the Future shall dimly rise and beckon — the ghastly deeds of the Past shall stretch out their skinny hands to push you forward! You shall not die unattended. Despair shall mock you. Agony shall offer her fiery cup, to your parched lips. Remorse shall feel for your heart, and rend it open.

Godly men shall breathe freer at your death, and utter thanksgiving when you are gone! Men shall place your grave-stone as a monument and testimony that a plague is stayed; no tear shall wet it, no mourner linger there! And, as borne on the blast, your guilty spirit whistles toward the gate of Hell, the hideous shrieks of those whom your hand has destroyed, shall pierce you — Hell's first welcome! In the bosom of that everlasting storm which rains perpetual misery in Hell, shall you, corrupter of youth — be forever hidden from our view! And may God wipe out the very thoughts of you from our memory!

Six Warnings

"The generation of the upright will be blessed. Wealth and riches are in his house, and his righteousness endures forever." Psalm 112:2-3

"He who gets riches, by unjust means, shall leave them in the midst of his days, and at the end shall be a fool." Jeremiah 17:11

When justly obtained, and rationally used — riches are called a gift of God, an evidence of his favor, and a great reward. When gathered unjustly, and corruptly used — wealth is pronounced a canker, a rust, a fire, a curse. There is no contradiction, then, when the Bible persuades to industry, and integrity, by a promise of riches; and then dissuades from wealth, as a terrible thing, destroying soul and body. Blessings are vindictive to abusers, and kind to rightful users; they serve us — or rule us. Fire warms our dwelling — or consumes it. Steam serves man — and also destroys him. Iron, in the plough, the sickle, the house, the ship, is indispensable. The assassin's knife, the cruel sword and the spear, are iron also.

The constitution of man, and of society, alike evinces the design of God. Both are made to be happier by the possession of riches — their full development and perfection are dependent, to a large extent, upon wealth. Without it, there can be neither books nor implements; neither commerce nor arts, neither towns nor cities. It is a folly to denounce that, a love of which God has placed in man by a constitutional faculty; that, with which he has associated high grades of happiness; that, which has motives touching every faculty of the mind.

Wealth is an Artist — by its patronage men are encouraged to paint, to carve, to design, to build and adorn. Wealth is a master-mechanic — and inspires man to invent, to discover, to apply, to forge, and to fashion. Wealth is a Gardener — and under its influence men rear the flock, till the earth, plant the vineyard, the field, the orchard, and the garden. Wealth is a manufacturer — and teaches men to card, to spin, to weave, to color and dress all useful fabrics. Wealth is a Merchant — and sends forth ships, and fills ware-houses with their returning cargoes gathered from every zone. Wealth is the scholar's patron — it sustains his leisure, rewards his labor, builds the college, and gathers the library.

Is a man weak? — he can buy the strong. Is he ignorant? — the learned will serve his wealth. Is he crude of speech? — he may procure the advocacy of the eloquent. The rich cannot buy honor — but honorable places, they can; they cannot purchase nobility — but they may its titles. Money cannot buy freshness of heart — but it can every luxury which tempts to enjoyment. Laws are its body-guard, and no earthly power may safely defy it; either while running in the swift channels of commerce, or reposing in the reservoirs of ancient families.

Here is an astonishing thing — that gold, an inert metal, which neither thinks, nor feels, nor stirs — can set the whole world to thinking, planning, running, digging, fashioning, and drives on the sweaty mass with never-ending labors!

Avarice seeks gold, not to build or buy therewith; not to clothe or feed itself; not to make it an instrument of wisdom, of skill, of friendship, or religion. Avarice seeks it — to heap it up; to walk around the pile, and gloat upon it;

to fondle, and court, to kiss and hug the darling stuff to the end of life, with the homage of idolatry.

Pride seeks it — for it gives power, and place, and titles, and exalts its possessor above his fellows. To be a thread in the fabric of life, just like any other thread, hoisted up and down by the treddle, played across by the shuttle, and woven tightly into the piece, this may suit humility — but not pride.

Vanity seeks it — what else can give it costly clothing, and rare ornaments, and stately dwellings, and showy equipage, and attract admiring eyes to its gaudy colors and costly jewels?

Taste seeks it — because by it, may be had whatever is beautiful, or refining, or instructive. What leisure has poverty for study, and how can it collect books, manuscripts, pictures, statues, coins, or curiosities?

Love seeks it — to build a home full of delights for father, wife or child; and, wisest of all,

Religion seeks it — to make it the messenger and servant of benevolence, to need, to suffering, and to ignorance.

What a sight does the busy world present, as of a great workshop, where hope and fear, love and pride, and lust, and pleasure, and avarice, separate or in partnership — drive on the universal race for wealth! Delving in the mine, digging in the earth, sweltering at the forge, plying the shuttle, ploughing the waters; in houses, in shops, in stores, on the mountain-side, or in the valley; by skill, by labor, by thought, by craft, by force, by traffic; all men, in all places, by all labors, fair and unfair, the world around, busy, busy; ever searching for wealth — that wealth may supply their pleasures.

As every taste and inclination may receive its gratification through riches, the universal and often fierce pursuit of it arises, not from the single impulse of avarice — but from the impulse of the whole mind; and on this very account, its pursuits should be more exactly regulated.

Let me set up a warning over against the special dangers which lie along the Road To RICHES.

I. I warn you against thinking that riches necessarily confer happiness; and that poverty always brings unhappiness. Do not begin life supposing that you shall be heart-rich, when you are purse-rich. A man's happiness depends primarily upon his disposition; if that is good — riches will bring pleasure; but only vexation — if his disposition is evil.

> To lavish money upon shining trifles,
> to make an idol of one's self for fools to gaze at,
> to rear mansions beyond our needs,
> to garnish them for display and not for use,
> to chatter through the heartless rounds of pleasure,
> to lounge, to gape, to simper and giggle
>   — can wealth make Vanity happy by such folly?

If wealth descends upon AVARICE — does it confer happiness? It blights the heart, as autumnal fires ravage the prairies! The eye glows with greedy cunning, conscience shrivels, the light of love goes out, and the wretch moves amidst his coin no better, no happier — than a loathsome reptile in a mine of gold. A dreary fire of self-love burns in the bosom of the avaricious rich, as a hermit's flame in a ruined temple of the desert. The fire is kindled for no deity, and is odorous with no incense — but only warms the shivering hermit.

Wealth will do little for LUST — but to hasten its corruption. There is no more happiness in a foul heart — than there is health in a pestilent morass. Satisfaction is not made out of such stuff as fighting carousals, obscene revelry, and midnight orgies. An alligator, gorging or swollen with surfeit and basking in the sun — has the same happiness which riches bring to the man who eats to gluttony, drinks to drunkenness, and sleeps to stupidity.

But riches indeed bless that heart whose almoner is Benevolence. If the taste is refined, if the affections are pure, if conscience is honest, if charity listens to the needy, and generosity relieves them; if the public-spirited hand fosters all that embellishes and all that ennobles society — then is the rich man happy.

On the other hand, do not suppose that all poverty is a waste and howling wilderness. There is a poverty of vice — base, loathsome, covered with all the sores of depravity. There is a poverty of indolence — where virtues sleep, and passions fret and bicker. There is a poverty which despondency makes — a deep dungeon, in which the victim wears hopeless chains. May God save you from that! There is a spiteful and venomous poverty — in which base and cankered hearts, repairing none of their own losses, spit at others' prosperity, and curse the rich — themselves doubly cursed by their own hearts.

But there is a contented poverty — in which industry and peace rule; and a joyful hope, which looks out into another world where riches shall neither fly nor fade. This poverty may possess an independent mind, a heart ambitious of usefulness, a hand quick to sow the seed of other men's happiness, and find its own joy in their enjoyment. If a serene age finds you in such poverty, it is such a wilderness, if it be a wilderness, as that in which God led his chosen people, and on which he rained every day a heavenly manna.

If God opens to your feet the way to wealth, enter it cheerfully; but remember that riches will either bless or curse you — as your own heart determines. But if circumscribed by necessity, you are still indigent, after all your industry, do not scorn poverty. There is often in the hut, more dignity — than in the palace. There is often more satisfaction in the poor man's scanty fare — than in the rich man's satiety.

II. Men are warned in the Bible against making haste to be rich. "He who hastens to be rich has an evil eye, and considers not that poverty shall come upon him!" This is spoken, not of the alacrity of enterprise — but of the precipitancy of avarice. That is an evil eye which leads a man into trouble by incorrect vision. When a man seeks to prosper by crafty tricks instead of careful industry; when a man's inordinate covetousness pushes him across all lines of honesty that he may sooner clutch the prize; when gambling speculation would reap where it had not strewn; when men gain riches by crimes — there is an Evil Eye, which guides them through a specious prosperity, to inevitable ruin!

So dependent is success upon patient industry, that he who seeks it otherwise, tempts his own ruin. A young lawyer, unwilling to wait for that practice which rewards a good reputation, or unwilling to earn that reputation by severe application, rushes through all the dirty paths of chicanery to a hasty prosperity; and he rushes out of it, by the dirtier paths of discovered villainy. A young politician, scarcely waiting until the law allows him, sturdily begs for that popularity which he should have patiently earned. In the ferocious conflicts of political life, cunning, intrigue, falsehood, slander, vituperative violence, at first sustain his pretensions — and at last demolish them. It is thus in all the ways of traffic, in all the arts, and trades. That prosperity which grows like the mushroom — is as poisonous as the mushroom! Few men are destroyed — but many destroy themselves.

When God sends wealth to bless men — he sends it gradually like a gentle rain. When God sends riches to punish men — they come tumultuously, like a roaring torrent, tearing up landmarks and sweeping all before them in promiscuous ruin. Almost every evil which environs the path to wealth, springs from that criminal haste which substitutes adroitness for industry, and trick for toil.

III. Let me warn you against Covetousness. "You shall not covet," is the law by which God sought to bless a favorite people. Covetousness is greediness of money. The Bible meets it with significant woes, by God's hatred, by solemn warnings, by denunciations, by exclusion from Heaven! This financial gluttony comes upon the competitors for wealth insidiously. At first, business is only a means of paying for our pleasures. Vanity soon whets the appetite for money, to sustain her parade and competition, to gratify her jealousies. Pride throws in fuel for a brighter flame. Vindictive hatreds often augment the passion, until the whole soul glows as a fervent furnace, and the body is driven as a boat whose ponderous engine trembles with the utmost energy of steam.

Covetousness is unprofitable. It defeats its own purposes. It breeds restless daring, where it is dangerous to venture. It works the mind to fever, so that its judgments are not cool, nor its calculations calm. Greed of money is like fire; the more fuel it has — the hotter it burns. Everything conspires to intensify the heat. Loss excites by desperation, and gain by exhilaration. When there is fever in the blood, there is fire on the brain; and courage turns to rashness, and rashness runs to ruin.

Covetousness breeds misery. The sight of houses better than our own, of dress beyond our means, of jewels costlier than we may wear, of stately equipage, and rare curiosities beyond our reach — these hatch the viper brood of covetous thoughts; vexing the poor — who would be rich; tormenting the rich — who would be richer. The covetous man pines to see pleasure; is sad in the presence of cheerfulness; and the joy of the world is his sorrow — because all the happiness of others is not his. I do not wonder that God abhors him! He inspects his heart, as he would a cave full of foul birds, or a nest of rattling reptiles, and loathes the sight of its crawling tenants! To the covetous man, life is a nightmare, and God lets him wrestle with it as best he may. Mammon might build its palace on such a heart, and Pleasure bring all its revelry there, and Honor all its garlands — it would be like pleasures in a sepulcher, and garlands on a tomb.

The creed of the greedy man is brief and consistent; and unlike other creeds, is both subscribed and believed. The chief end of man is to glorify Gold and enjoy him forever.

Life is a time afforded man to grow rich in;
death, the winding up of speculations;
Heaven, a mart with golden streets;
Hell, a place where shiftless men are punished with everlasting poverty.

God searched among the beasts for a fit emblem of contempt, to describe the end of a covetous prince: He shall be buried with the burial of an Donkey, drawn and cast forth beyond the gates of Jerusalem. He whose heart is turned to greediness, who sweats through life under the load of labor only to heap up money, and dies without private usefulness, or a record of public service — is no better, in God's estimation, than a pack-horse — a mule — an donkey; a creature for burdens, to be beaten, and worked and killed, and dragged off by another like him, abandoned to the birds and forgotten.

He is buried with the burial of an donkey! This is the Miser's Epitaph — and yours, Young Man! if you earn it by covetousness!

IV. I warn you against Selfishness. Of riches it is written: "There is no good in them, but for a man to rejoice and to do good in his life." If men selfishly absorb their property, it parches the heart so that it will not give forth blossoms and fruits — but only thorns and thistles. If men radiate and reflect upon others some rays of the prosperity which shines upon themselves — then wealth is not only harmless — but full of advantage.

The thoroughfares of wealth are crowded by a throng who jostle, and thrust, and conflict — like men in the tumult of a battle. The rules which crafty old men breathe into the ears of the young, are full of selfish wisdom —

teaching them that the chief end of man is to harvest and to hoard. Their life is made obedient to a scale of preferences graded from a sordid experience; a scale which has poverty for one extreme, and stinginess for the other; and the virtues are ranked between them as they are relatively fruitful in physical thrift. Every crevice of the heart is caulked with stingy maxims — so that no precious drop of wealth may leak out through inadvertent generosities. Indeed, generosity and all its company, are thought to be little better than pilfering pick-locks, against whose wiles the heart is prepared, like a coin-vault, with iron-clenched walls of stone, and impenetrable doors. Mercy, pity, and sympathy — are vagrant fowls; and that they may not scale the fence between a man and his neighbors, their wings are clipped by the miser's master-maxim — Charity Begins At Home. It certainly stays there.

    The habit of regarding men as dishonest rivals, dries up, also, the kindlier feelings. A shrewd trafficker must watch his fellows, be suspicious of their offers, vigilant of their movements, and jealous of their pledges. The world's way is a very crooked way, and a very deceitful one. Its travelers creep by stealth, or walk craftily, or glide, in concealments, or appear in specious guises. He who stands watching among men, to pluck his advantage from their hands, or to lose it by their wiles — comes at length to regard all men as either enemies or instruments. Of course he thinks it fair to strip an enemy; and just as fair to use an instrument. Men are no more to him than bales, boxes, or goods — mere matters of business. If he ever relaxes his commercial rigidity to indulge in the fictions of poetry, it is when, perhaps on Sundays or at a funeral, he talks quite prettily about friendship, and generosity, and philanthropy. The tightest ship may leak in a storm, and an unbartered penny may escape from this man, when the surprise of the solicitation gives no time for thought.

The heart cannot wholly petrify without some honest revulsions. Opiates are administered to it. This businessman tells his heart that it is beset by unscrupulous enemies; that beneficent virtues are doors to let them in; that liberality is bread given to one's foes; and selfishness only self-defense. At the same time, he enriches the future with generous promises. While he is getting rich, he cannot afford to be liberal; but when once he is rich, ah! how liberal he means to be! As though habits could be unbuckled like a belt, and were not rather steel-bands riveted, defying the edge of any man's resolution, and clasping the heart with invincible servitude!

Thorough selfishness destroys or paralyzes enjoyment. A heart made selfish by the contest for wealth, is like a citadel stormed in war. The banner of victory waves over dilapidated walls, desolate chambers, and magazines riddled with artillery. Men, covered with sweat, and begrimed with toil — expect to find joy in a heart reduced by selfishness to a smouldering heap of ruins.

I warn every aspirant for wealth, against the infernal canker of selfishness. It will eat out of the heart with the fire of Hell, or bake it harder than a stone! The heart of avaricious old age stands like a bare rock in a bleak wilderness, and there is no rod of authority, nor incantation of pleasure, which can draw from it one crystal drop to quench the raging thirst for satisfaction. But listen not to my words alone; hear the solemn voice of God, pronouncing doom upon the selfish: "Your wealth has rotted, and moths have eaten your clothes. Your gold and silver are corroded. Their corrosion will testify against you and eat your flesh like fire!"

5. I warn you against seeking wealth by Covert Dishonesty. The everlasting plea of petty fraud or open dishonesty, is, its necessity or profitableness.

But it is neither necessary — nor profitable. The hope is a deception, and the excuse a lie. The severity of competition affords no reason for dishonesty in word or deed. Competition is fair — but not all methods of competition. A mechanic may compete with a mechanic, by rising earlier, by greater industry, by greater skill, more punctuality, greater thoroughness, by employing better materials; by a more scrupulous fidelity to promises, and by facility in accommodation. A merchant may study to excel competitors, by a better selection of goods, by more obliging manners, by more rigid honesty, by a better knowledge of the market, by better taste in the arrangement of his goods. Industry, honesty, kindness, taste, genius and skill — are the only materials of all rightful competition!

But whenever you have exerted all your knowledge, all your skill, all your industry, with long continued patience and without success, then, it is clear, not that you may proceed to employ trick and cunning — but that you must stop. God has put before you a bound which no man may overleap. There may be the appearance of gain on the knavish side of the wall of honor. Traps are always baited with food sweet to the taste of the intended victim; and Satan is too crafty a trapper not to scatter the pitfall of dishonesty with some shining particles of gold.

But what if fraud were necessary to permanent success? Will you take success upon such terms? I perceive, too often, that young men regard the argument as ended, when they prove to themselves that they cannot be rich without deceit. Very well — then be poor! But if you prefer money to honor — you may well swear fidelity to the villain's law! If it is not base and detestable to gain by equivocation — then neither is it by lying; and if not by lying — then neither is it by stealing; and if not by stealing — then neither by robbery or murder. Will you tolerate the loss of honor and honesty, for the sake of profit?

For exactly this, Judas betrayed Christ, and Benedict Arnold his country. Because deceit is the only way to gain some pleasure — then . . .

may a wife yield her honor?
may a politician sell himself?
may a statesman barter his counsel?
may a judge take bribes?
may a juryman forswear himself?
or a witness commit perjury?

Then virtues are marketable commodities, and may be hung up, like meat in the shambles, or sold at auction to the highest bidder.

Who can afford a victory — if gained by a defeat of his virtue? What prosperity can compensate the plundering of a man's heart? "A good name is rather to be chosen than great riches" — sooner or later every man will find it so.

With what dismay would Esau have sorrowed for a lost birthright, had he lost also the pitiful porridge for which he sold it? With what double despair would Judas have clutched at death, if he had not obtained even the thirty pieces of silver which were to pay his infamy? And with what utter confusion will all dishonest men, who were learning from the Devil to defraud other men, find at length, that he was giving his most finished lesson of deception — by cheating them! and making poverty and disgrace the only fruit of the lies and frauds which were framed for profit! Getting treasure by a lying tongue, is a vanity tossed to and fro by those who seek damnation!

Men have only looked upon the beginning of a career, when they pronounce upon the profitableness of dishonesty. Many a ship goes gaily out of harbor — which never returns again. That only is a good voyage — which brings home the richly-freighted ship. God explicitly declares that an inevitable curse of dishonesty, shall fall upon the criminal himself, or upon his children. He who by usury, and unjust gain, increases his substance — he shall gather it for him who will pity the poor. His children are far from safety, and they are crushed in the gate. Neither is there any to deliver them — the robber swallows up their substance.

Iniquities, whose end is dark as midnight, are permitted to open bright as the morning; the most poisonous bud unfolds with brilliant colors. So the threshold of perdition is burnished until it glows like the gate of paradise. "There is a way which seems right unto a man — but the ends thereof are the ways of death!" This end is dishonesty described to the full. At first you look down upon a smooth and verdant path covered with flowers, perfumed with fragrances, and overhung with fruits and grateful shade. Its long perspective is illusive; for it ends quickly in a precipice, over which you pitch into irretrievable ruin!

For the sources of this inevitable disaster, we need look no further than the effect of dishonesty upon a man's own mind. The difference between cunning and wisdom — is the difference between acting by the certain and immutable laws of nature, and acting by the shifts of temporary expedients. An honest man puts his prosperity upon the broad current of those laws which govern the world. A crafty man means to pry between them, to steer across them, to take advantage of them. An honest man steers by God's chart; and a dishonest man by his own. Which is the most liable to perplexities and fatal mistakes of judgment? Wisdom steadily ripens to the end; cunning is worm-bitten, and soon drops from the tree.

I could repeat the names of many men, (every village has such, and they swarm in cities,) who are skillful, indefatigable — but audaciously dishonest; and for a time, they seemed going straight forward to the realm of wealth. But I never knew a single one to avoid ultimate ruin. Men who act under dishonest passions — are like men riding fierce horses. It is not always with the rider — when or where he shall stop. If for his sake, the steed dashes wildly on while the road is smooth; so, turning suddenly into a rough and dangerous way, the rider must go madly forward for the steed's sake — now chafed, his mettle up, his eye afire, and beast and burden like a bolt speeding through the air, until some bound or sudden fall tumble both to the ground — a crushed and mangled mass!

A man pursuing plain ends by honest means, may be troubled on every side — yet not distressed; perplexed — but not in despair; persecuted — but not forsaken; cast down — but not destroyed. But those who pursue their advantage by a round of dishonesties, "when fear comes as a desolation, and destruction as a whirlwind, when distress and anguish come upon them — shall eat of the fruit of their own way, and be filled with their own devices; for the turning away of the simple shall slay them; and the prosperity of fools shall destroy them."

6. The Bible overflows with warnings to those who gain wealth by violent extortion, or by any flagrant villainy. Some men stealthily slip the possessions of the poor from under them. Some beguile the simple and heedless, of their inheritance. Some tyrannize over ignorance, and extort from it, its fair domains. Some steal away the senses, and intoxicate the mind — the more readily and largely to cheat; some set their traps in all the dark places of men's adversity, and prowl for wrecks all along the shores, on which men's fortunes go to pieces. Men will take advantage of extreme misery, to wring it with more griping tortures, and compel it to the extreme sacrifices; and stop only when no more can be borne by the sufferer, or nothing more extracted by the usurer. The earth is as full of these avaricious monsters — as the tropical forests are of beasts of prey. But amid all the lions, and tigers, and hyenas — is seen the stately bulk of three huge Behemoths.

The first Behemoth is that incarnate fiend who navigates the ocean to traffic in human slavery, and freight with the groans and tears of agony. Distant shores are sought with cords and manacles; villages surprised with torch and sword; and the loathsome ship swallows what the sword and the fire have spared. By night and day the voyage speeds, and the storm spares wretches more relentless than itself. The wind wafts and the sun lights the path for a ship whose log is written in blood. Hideous profits, dripping red, even at this hour, lure these infernal miscreants to their remorseless errands. The thirst of gold inspires such courage, skill, and cunning vigilance — that the thunders of four allied navies cannot sink the infamous fleet.

What wonder! Just such a Behemoth of rapacity stalks among us, and fattens on the blood of our sons. Men there are, who, without a pang or gleam of remorse, will coolly wait for character to rot, and health to sink, and means to melt — that they may suck up the last drop of the victim's blood. Our streets are full of reeling wretches whose bodies and manhood and souls have been crushed and put to the press, that monsters might wring out of them a wine for their infernal thirst. The agony of midnight massacre, the frenzy of the ship's dungeon, the living death of the passage, the wails of separation, and the dismal torpor of hopeless servitude — are these found only in the piracy of the slave trade? They all are among us! worse assassinations! worse dragging to a prison-ship! worse groans ringing from the stinking ship! worse separations of families! worse bondage of intemperate men, enslaved by that most inexorable of all taskmasters — sexual habit!

The third Behemoth is seen lurking among the Indian savages, and bringing the arts of learning, and the skill of civilization, to aid in plundering the debauched barbarian. The cunning, murdering, scalping Indian — is no match for the Christian whiteman. Compared with the midnight knavery of men reared in schools, rocked by religion, tempered and taught by the humane institutions of liberty and civilization — all the craft of the savage is as twilight. Vast estates have been accumulated, without having an honest farthing in them. Our Penitentiaries might be sent to school to the Treaty-grounds and Council-grounds. Smugglers and swindlers might humble themselves in the presence of Indian traders. All the crimes against property known to our laws, nourish with unnatural vigor; and some, unknown to civilized villainy!

To swindle ignorance, to overreach simplicity, to lie without scruple to any extent; to tempt the savages to rob each other, and to receive their plunder; to sell goods at incredible prices to the sober Indian, then to intoxicate him, and steal them all back by a sham bargain, to be sold again, and stolen again; to employ falsehood, lust, threats, whisky, and even the knife and the pistol; in short to consume the Indian's substance by every vice and crime possible to an unprincipled heart inflamed with an insatiable rapacity, unwatched by Justice, and unrestrained by Law — this it is to be an Indian Trader!

I would rather inherit the center of Vesuvius, or make my bed in Mount Etna, than own those estates which have been scalped off from human beings as the hunter strips a beaver of its fur. Of all these, of all who gain possessions by extortion and robbery — never let yourself be envious! "For I envied the proud when I saw them prosper despite their wickedness. They seem to live such painless lives; their bodies are so healthy and strong. They don't have troubles like other people; they're not plagued with problems like everyone else. They wear pride like a jeweled necklace and clothe themselves with cruelty. When I tried to understand all this, it was oppressive to me until I entered the sanctuary of God; then I understood their final destiny. Surely you place them on slippery ground; you cast them down to ruin. How suddenly are they destroyed, completely swept away by terrors!"

I would not bear their heart, who have so made money — were the world a solid globe of gold, and mine! I would not stand for them in the judgment — were every star of

Heaven a realm of riches, and mine. I would not walk with them to the burning fires of Hell, to bear their torment, and utter their groans — for the throne of God itself.

Let us hear the conclusion of the whole matter:
Riches got by deceit, cheat no man so much as the getter!
Riches bought with guile — God will pay for with vengeance!
Riches got by fraud — are dug out of one's own heart, and destroy the mine!
Unjust riches — curse the owner in getting, in keeping, in transmitting!
They curse his children in their father's memory, in their own wasteful habits, in drawing around them all bad men to be their companions.

While I do not discourage your search for wealth, I warn you that it is not a cruise upon level seas, and under kind skies. You advance where ten thousand are broken in pieces, before they reach the mart; where those who reach it are worn out by their labors, and past enjoying their riches. You seek a land pleasant to the sight — but dangerous to the feet; a land of fragrant winds — which lull to security; of golden fruits — which are poisonous; of glorious hues — which dazzle and mislead.

You may be rich and be pure — but it will cost you a great struggle. You may be rich and go to Heaven — but ten, doubtless, will sink beneath their riches, where one breaks through them to Heaven. If you have entered this shining way — begin to look for snares and traps. Go not careless of your danger, and provoking it. See, on every side of you, how many there are who seal God's word with their blood!

"But people who long to be rich fall into temptation and are trapped by many foolish and harmful desires that plunge them into ruin and destruction. For the love of money is the root of all kinds of evil. And some people, craving money, have wandered from the true faith and pierced themselves with many sorrows!" 1 Timothy 6:9-10

Industry and Idleness

"Give us this day our daily bread." Matthew 6:11

"For even when we were with you, we gave you this rule: 'If a man will not work, he shall not eat!' We hear that some among you are idle. They are not busy; they are busybodies. Such people we command and urge in the Lord Jesus Christ to settle down and earn the bread they eat!" 2 Thessalonians 3:10-12.

The bread which we ask from God — he gives us through our own industry. Prayer sows it — and Industry reaps it.

INDUSTRY is the habitual activity in some useful pursuit. So, not only inactivity — but also all activities without the design of usefulness, are of the nature of IDLENESS. The supine sluggard is no more indolent than the bustling do-nothing. Men may walk much, and read much, and talk much, and pass the day without an unoccupied moment, and yet be substantially idle; because Industry requires, at least, the intention of usefulness. But gadding, gazing, lounging, mere pleasure-mongering, reading for the relief of boredom — these are as useless as sleeping, or dozing, or the stupidity of a glutton.

There are many grades of idleness; and veins of it run through the most industrious life. We shall indulge in some descriptions of the various classes of idlers, and leave the reader to judge, if he is an indolent man — to which class he belongs.

1. The lazy man. He is of a very ancient pedigree; for his family is minutely described by Solomon: "How long will you sleep, O sluggard? when will you awake out of sleep?" This is the language of impatience; the speaker has been trying to awaken him — pulling, pushing, rolling him over, and shouting in his ear; but all to no purpose. He soliloquizes, whether it is possible for the man ever to wake up! At length, the sleeper drawls out a dozing petition to be let alone: "Yet a little sleep, a little slumber, a little folding of the hands to sleep;" and the last words confusedly break into a snore — that somnolent lullaby of repose!

Long ago the birds have finished their morning prayers, the sun has advanced full high, the dew has gone from the grass, and the labors of Industry are far in progress — when our sluggard, awakened by his very efforts to maintain sleep, slowly emerges to perform life's great duty of eating — with him, second only in importance to sleep. And now, well rested, and suitably nourished — surely he will abound in labor. Nay, the sluggard will not plough by reason of the cold weather. It is yet early spring; there is ice in the north; and the winds are hearty — his tender skin shrinks from exposure, and he waits for milder days — envying the residents of tropical climates, where cold never comes, and harvests wave spontaneously.

He is valiant at sleeping all the morning; but for other courage, the slothful man says, "There is a lion outside! I shall be slain in the street!" He has not been out to see; but he heard a noise, and resolutely betakes himself to prudence. Under so thriving a manager, so alert in the morning, so busy through the day, and so enterprising — we might anticipate the thrift of his farm, "I went past the field of the sluggard, past the vineyard of the man who lacks judgment; thorns had come up everywhere, the ground was covered with weeds, and the stone wall was in ruins!"

To complete the picture, only one thing more is needed — a description of his house — and then we should have, at one view — the lazy man, his farm, and house. Solomon has given us that also: "If a man is lazy, the rafters sag; if his hands are idle, the house leaks!" Let all this be put together, and possibly some reader may find an unpleasant resemblance to his own affairs!

He sleeps long and late, he wakes to slothfulness, with indolent eyes sleepily rolling over neglected work; neglected because it is too cold in spring, and too hot in summer, and too laborious at all times — a great coward in danger, and therefore very boasting in safety. His lands run to waste, his fences are dilapidated, his crops are chiefly of weeds and brambles; his house is sagging, the side leaning over as if wishing, like its owner, to lie down to sleep; the chimney tumbling down; the roof breaking in, with moss and grass sprouting in its crevices; the well without pump or cover, a trap for their children. This is the very castle of Indolence!

2. Another idler as useless — but vastly more active than the last, attends closely to everyone's business — except his own! His wife earns the children's bread — and his; she procures her own clothing — and his; she procures the wood; she procures the water. While he, with hands in his pocket, is busy watching the building of a neighbor's barn; or advising another how to trim and train his vines. Or he has heard of sickness in a friend's family, and is there, to suggest a hundred cures, and to do everything but to help. He is a spectator of all the sports matches in town.

He knows all the stories of all the families who live in the village. If he can catch a stranger at the tavern in a rainy day, he pours out a strain of information, a pattering of words, as thick as the rain-drops out side. He has good advice to everybody, how to save, how to make money, how to do everything. He can tell the saddle-maker about his trade; he gives advice to the blacksmith about his work, suggests improvements, advises this paint or that varnish, criticizes the finish, or praises the trimmings. He is a ravenous reader of newspapers, almanacs, and magazines. And with scraps of history and mutilated anecdotes — he faces the very school-master, and gives up only to the articulateness of the oily-tongued village lawyer — few have the hardihood to match him.

And thus every day he bustles through his multifaceted idleness, and completes his circle of visits, as regularly as the hands of a clock visit each figure on the dial-plate. But alas! the clock forever tells man the useful lesson of time passing steadily away — and returning never. But what useful thing do these busy-buzzing-idlers perform?

3. We introduce another idler. He follows no job; he only follows those who do. Sometimes he sweeps along the streets, with all-important gait; sometimes perfumes it with the unpleasant odors of tobacco. He also frequents sunny benches, or breezy piazzas. His business is to see. His desire to be seen, and no one fails to see him — so gaudily dressed, his hat sitting aslant upon a wilderness of hair, like a bird half startled from its nest, and every thread arranged to provoke attention. He is a man of honor — not that he keeps his word or shrinks from baseness. He defrauds his laundress, his tailor, and his landlord. He drinks and smokes at other men's expense. He gambles and swears,

and fights — when he is too drunk to be afraid; but still he is a man of honor, for he has whiskers and looks fierce, wears a large bushy moustache with hair growing down the sides of the mouth, and says, "Upon my honor, sir!" "Do you doubt my honor, sir?"

Thus he appears by day. By night he does not appear; he may be dimly seen flitting around; his voice may be heard loud in the carousal of some tavern — or above the songs and uproar of a midnight return, staggering home.

4. The next of this brotherhood of idlers excites our pity. He began life most thriftily; for his rising family he was gathering an ample subsistence; but, involved in other men's affairs, he went down in their ruin. Late in life he begins once more, and at length, just secure of an easy competence — his ruin is compassed again. He sits down quietly under it, complains of no one, envies no one, refuses the cup, and is even more pure in morals, than in better days. He moves on from day to day, as one who walks under a spell — it is the spell of despondency, which nothing can disenchant or arouse. He neither seeks work nor refuses it. He wanders among men a dreaming gazer, poorly clad, always kind, always irresolute, able to plan nothing for himself, nor to execute what others have planned for him. He lives and he dies a discouraged man, and the most harmless and excusable of all idlers.

5. I have not mentioned the fashionable idler — whose riches defeat every object for which God gave him birth. He has a fine form, and manly beauty, and the chief end of life is to display them. With notable diligence, he ransacks the market for rare and curious clothes, for costly jewelry, and chains, and rings. A poorly-fitted coat is the unpardonable sin of his creed. He meditates upon fine

clothes, employs a profound discrimination in selecting a hat, or a vest, and adopts his conclusions upon the tastefulness of a button or a neck-tie, with the deliberation of a statesman.

Thus dressed up, he saunters in fashionable galleries, or flaunts his stylish equipage, or parades the streets with silly belles, or delights their itching ears with compliments of flattery, or with choicely culled scandals. He is a reader of fictions, a player of cards, and is especially conspicuous in games. Mirthful and frivolous, rich and useless, polished until the enamel is worn off — his whole life serves only to make him an animated puppet of pleasure. He is as corrupt in imagination — as he is refined in manners. He is as selfish in private — as he is generous in public; and even what he gives to another, is given for his own sake. He worships where fashion worships — today at the theater, tomorrow at the church, as either exhibits the whitest hand, or the most polished actor. A gaudy, busy and indolent butterfly — he flutters without industry from flower to flower, until summer closes, and frosts sting him, and he sinks down and dies, unthought of and unremembered.

6. One other portrait should be drawn of a business man, who wishes to exist by his occupation, while he attends to everything else. If a sporting club meets — he must go. He has set his fishing-line in every hole in the river, and dozed in a summer day under every tree along its bank. He rejoices in a riding party — a sleigh-ride — a summer frolic — a winter's glee. He is everybody's friend — universally good-natured — forever busy where it will do him no good, and remiss where his interests require activity. He takes amusement for his main business — which other men employ as a relaxation. And the serious labor of life, which other men are mainly employed in —

he knows only as a relaxation. After a few years he fails, his good nature is somewhat clouded, and as age sobers his buoyancy, without repairing his profitless habits — he soon sinks to a lower grade of laziness, and to ruin.

It would be endless to describe the wiles of idleness — how it insidiously creeps in upon men, how secretly it mingles with their pursuits, how much time it purloins from the scholar, from the professional man, and from the artisan. It steals minutes, it clips off the edges of hours, and at length takes possession of days. Where it has its will — it sinks and drowns employment. But where necessity, or ambition, or duty resists such extremes — then indolence makes labor heavy; scatters the attention; puts us to our tasks with wandering thoughts, with irresolute purpose, and with dreamy visions. Thus when it may — it plucks out hours and rules over them; and where this may not be — it lurks around them to impede the sway of industry, and turn her seeming toils to subtle idleness.

Against so mischievous an enchantress — we should be duly armed. I shall, therefore, describe the advantages of Industry — and the evils of Indolence.

1. A hearty industry promotes happiness. Some men of the greatest industry, are unhappy from sourness of disposition; they are morose, or suspicious, or envious. Such qualities make happiness impossible under any circumstances.

Health is the platform on which all happiness must be built. Good appetite, good digestion, and good sleep — are the elements of health — and Industry confers them. As use polishes metals, so labor polishes the faculties, until the body performs its unimpeded functions with elastic cheerfulness and hearty enjoyment.

Buoyant spirits are an element of happiness — and activity produces them; but they fly away from sluggishness. Men's spirits are like water, which sparkles when it runs — but stagnates in still pools, and is mantled with green, and breeds corruption and filth.

The applause of conscience,
the self-respect of wholesome pride,
the consciousness of independence,
a manly joy of usefulness,
the consent of every faculty of the mind to one's occupation, and their gratification in it
— these constitute a happiness superior to the fever-flashes of vice in its brightest moments.

After an experience of ages, men should have learned that satisfaction is not the product of excess, or of indolence, or of luxury — but of industry, temperance, and usefulness! Every village has instances which ought to teach young men, that he who goes aside from the simplicity of nature, and the purity of virtue — to wallow in excesses of food or drink, or carousals — at length misses the goal of his life; and sinking with shattered body prematurely to a dishonored grave, mourns that he mistook exhilaration for satisfaction — and abandoned the very home of happiness, when he forsook the labors of useful Industry.

The poor man with Industry — is happier than the rich man in Idleness; for labor makes the one more manly — and riches unmans the other. The slave is often happier than the master, who is nearer undone by luxury — than his vassal by toil. Luxurious couches, plushy carpets from oriental looms, pillows of down, carriages contrived with cushions and springs to make motion imperceptible — is the indolent master of the rich. And often, happy is the slave who wove the carpet, the Indian who hunted the northern flock, and the servant who drives the pampered steeds! Let those who envy the mirthful revels of rich idlers, and pine for their masquerades, their escapades, and their operas — experience for a week the lassitude of their gluttony, the unarousable torpor of their life when not under a fiery stimulus, their desperate boredom, and restless somnolence — and they would gladly flee from their indolent haunts, as from a land of cursed enchantment!

2. Industry is the parent of thrift. In the overburdened states of Europe, the severest toil often only suffices to make life a wretched vacillation between food and famine; but in America, Industry is prosperity.

Although God has stored the world with an endless variety of riches for man's needs, he has made them all accessible only to Industry. The food we eat, the clothing which covers us, the house which protects — must be secured by diligence. To tempt man yet more to Industry — every product of the earth has a susceptibility of improvement; so that man not only obtains the gifts of nature at the price of labor — but these gifts become more precious as we bestow upon them greater skill and cultivation. The wheat and corn which crown our ample fields, were foods fit only for birds, before man perfected them by labor. The fruits of the forest and the hedge, scarcely tempting to extreme hunger — after human skill has dealt with them and transplanted them to the orchard and the garden, allure every sense with the richest colors, fragrances, and flavors. The world is full of sources which man is set to develop; and there is scarcely an assignable limit, to which the hand of skill and labor may not improve the powers of nature.

The scheming speculations of the last ten years have produced an aversion among the young, to the slow accumulations of ordinary Industry — and fired them with a conviction that shrewdness, cunning, and bold ventures, are a more manly way to wealth. There is a swarm of men, bred in the heats of adventurous times, whose thoughts scorn pennies and nickels, and who humble themselves to speak of dollars — hundreds and thousands are their words. They are men of great operations. Forty thousand dollars is a moderate profit of a single speculation. They mean to own the Bank; and to look down, before they die, upon moderately wealthy. The young farmer becomes almost ashamed to meet his schoolmate, whose stores line whole streets, whose stocks are in every bank and company, and whose increasing money is already well near inestimable. But if the butterfly derides the bee in summer — he was never known to do it in the stormy days of autumn.

Every few years, Commerce has its earthquakes, and the tall and toppling warehouses which haste ran up — are the first to be shaken down. The hearts of men fail them for fear; and the suddenly rich, made more suddenly poor — fill the land with their loud laments. But nothing strange has happened. When the whole story of commercial disasters is told, it is only found out that they, who slowly amassed the gains of useful Industry, built upon a rock; and they, who flung together the imaginary millions of commercial speculations, built upon the sand. When times grew dark, and the winds came, and the floods descended and beat upon them both — the rock sustained the one, and the shifting sand let down the other.

If a young man has no higher ambition in life than riches — then Industry — plain, rugged, brown-faced, homely clad, old-fashioned Industry — must be courted. Young men are pressed with a most unprofitable haste. They wish to reap — before they have ploughed or sown. Everything is driving at such a rapid rate, that they have become giddy. Laborious occupations are avoided. Money is to be earned in genteel leisure, with the help of fine clothes, and by the soft seductions of smooth hair and luxuriant whiskers.

Parents, equally wild, foster the delusion. Shall the promising lad be apprenticed to his uncle, the blacksmith? The sisters think the blacksmith so very smutty; the mother shrinks from the ungentility of his swarthy labor; the father, weighing the matter prudentially deeper, finds that a whole life had been spent in earning the uncle's property. These sagacious parents, wishing the tree to bear its fruit before it has ever blossomed — regard the long delay of industrious trades as a fatal objection to them. The son, then, must be a rich merchant, or a popular lawyer, or a broker; and these, only as the openings to business speculation.

Young business men are often educated in two very unthrifty species of contempt — a contempt for small gains, and a contempt for hard labor. To do one's own errands, to wheel one's own barrow, to be seen with a bundle, bag, or burden — is considered disreputable. Men are so sharp now-a-days, that they can compass by their shrewd heads — what their fathers used to do with their heads and hands.

3. Industry gives character and good reputation to the young. The reputable portions of society have maxims of prudence, by which the young are judged and admitted to their good opinion. Does he regard his word? Is he industrious? Is he economical? Is he free from immoral habits? The answer which a young man's conduct gives to these questions, settles his reception among good men. Experience has shown that the other good qualities of veracity, frugality, and modesty — are usually associated with industry. A prudent man would scarcely be persuaded that a listless, lounging fellow — would be economical or trust-worthy. An employer would judge wisely, that where there was little regard for time, or for occupation — there would be as little, upon temptation, for honesty or veracity. Pilferings of the till, and robberies, are fit deeds for idle clerks, and lazy apprentices. Industry and dishonesty are sometimes found associated; but men wonder at it, as at a strange thing. The epithets of society, which betoken its experience, are all in favor of Industry. Thus, the terms "a hard-working man;" "an industrious man;" "a laborious artisan;" are employed to mean, an honest man; a trustworthy man.

I may here, as well as anywhere, impart the secret of what is called good and bad luck. There are men who, supposing Providence to have an implacable spite against them, bemoan the misfortunes of their lives, in the poverty of a wretched old age. Luck forever ran against them — and for others. One with a good profession, lost his luck in the river, where he idled away his time a fishing, when he should have been in the office. Another, with a good trade, perpetually burnt up his luck by his hot temper, which provoked all his employers to fire him. Another, with a lucrative business, lost his luck by amazing diligence at everything but his business. Another, who steadily followed his trade — as steadily followed his bottle. Another, who was honest and constant to his work, erred by perpetual misjudgments — he lacked discretion. Hundreds lose their luck by expectant speculations; by trusting fraudulent men; and by dishonest gains.

A man never has good luck — who has a bad wife.

I never knew an early-rising, hard-working, prudent man, careful of his earnings, and strictly honest — who complained of bad luck. A good character, good habits, and iron industry — are impregnable to the assaults of all the bad luck which fools ever dreamed of. But when I see a ragamuffin, creeping out into the street late in the forenoon, with his hands stuck into his pockets, the rim of his hat turned up, and the crown knocked in — I know he has had bad luck — for the worst of all luck, is to be a sluggard, a knave, or a drunkard.

4. Industry is a substitute for Genius. Where one or more faculties exist in the highest state of development and activity — as the faculty of music in Mozart — invention in Fulton — idealism in Milton — we call their possessor a genius. But a genius is usually misunderstood to be a creature of such rare facility of mind — that he can do anything without labor. According to the popular notion — he learns without study, and knows without learning. He is eloquent without preparation; exact without calculation; and profound without reflection. While ordinary men toil for knowledge by reading, by comparison, and by minute research — a genius is supposed to receive it as the mind receives dreams. His mind is like a vast cathedral, through whose colored windows the sunlight streams, painting the aisles with the varied colors of brilliant pictures.

Such geniuses may exist. But so far as my observations have ascertained the species — they abound in academies, colleges, and actor societies; in village debating clubs; in coteries of young artists, and among young professional aspirants. They are to be known by a reserved air, excessive sensitiveness, and utter indolence; by very long hair, and very open shirt collars; by the reading of much wretched poetry, and the writing of much — yet more wretched; by being very conceited, very ostentatious, very disagreeable, and very useless — beings whom no man wants for friend, pupil, or companion!

The occupations of the truly great man, and of the common man, are necessarily, for the most part, the same; for the business of life is made up of minute affairs, requiring only judgment and diligence. A high order of intellect is required for the discovery and defense of truth — but this is an infrequent task. Those who enlarge the bounds of knowledge, must push out with bold adventure beyond the common walks of men. But only a few pioneers are needed for the largest armies, and a few profound men in each occupation may herald the advance of all the business of society.

The vast bulk of men are required to discharge the common duties of life; and they have less need of genius than of intellectual Industry and patient Enterprise. Young men should observe, that those who take the honors and emoluments of mechanical crafts, of commerce and of professional life — are rather distinguished for a sound judgment and a close application — than for a brilliant genius. In the ordinary business of life — Industry can do anything which Genius can do; and very many things which it cannot. Genius is usually impatient of application, irritable, scornful of men's dullness, squeamish at petty disgusts — it loves a conspicuous place, a short work, and a large reward. It loathes . . .

>   the sweat of toil,
>   the vexations of life,
>   and the dull burden of care.

Industry has a firmer muscle, is less annoyed by delays and repulses; and, like water, bends itself to the shape of the soil over which it flows; and if checked, will not rest — but accumulates, and mines a passage beneath, or seeks a side-track, or rises above and overflows the obstruction. What Genius performs at one impulse — Industry gains by a succession of blows. In ordinary matters, they differ only in rapidity of execution, and are upon one level before men — who see the result, but not the process.

It is admirable to know that those things which in skill, in art, and in learning, the world has been unwilling to let die, have not only been the conceptions of genius — but the products of toil. The masterpieces of antiquity, as well in literature, as in art — are known to have received their exquisite finish, from an almost incredible continuance of labor upon them. I do not remember a book in all the departments of learning, nor a scrap in literature, nor a work in all the schools of art, from which its author has derived a permanent renown, that is not known to have been long and patiently elaborated.

Genius needs Industry — as much as Industry needs Genius. If only Milton's imagination could have conceived his visions, his consummate industry only could have carved the immortal lines which enshrine them. If only Newton's mind could reach out to the secrets of Nature, even his could only do it by the severest toil. The works of Bacon are not midsummer-night dreams — but, like coral islands, they have risen from the depths of truth, and formed their broad surfaces above the ocean by the minutest accretions of persevering labor. The conceptions of Michelangelo would have perished like a night's phantasy, had not his industry given them permanence.

From enjoying the pleasant walks of Industry — we turn reluctantly to explore the paths of Indolence.

All degrees of Indolence incline a man to rely upon others — and not upon himself; to eat their bread — and not his own. His carelessness — is somebody's loss; his neglect — is somebody's downfall; his promises — are a perpetual stumbling block to all who trust them. If he borrows — the article remains borrowed; if he begs and gets — it is as the letting out of waters — no one knows when it will stop. He . . .

> spoils your work;
> disappoints your expectations;
> exhausts your patience;
> eats up your substance;
> abuses your confidence; and
> hangs a dead weight upon all your plans!

The very best thing an honest man can do with a lazy man, is to get rid of him! Solomon says: "Though you grind a fool in a mortar, grinding him like grain with a pestle — you will not remove his folly from him!" He does not mention what kind of a fool he meant; but as he speaks of a fool by preeminence, I take it for granted he meant a lazy man; and I am the more inclined to the opinion, from another expression of his experience: "As vinegar to the teeth and smoke to the eyes — so is a sluggard to those who send him!"

Indolence is a great spendthrift. An indolently inclined young man, can neither make nor keep property. I have Scriptural authority for this: "One who is slack in his work — is brother to one who is a great waster!"

When Satan would put ordinary men to a crop of mischief, like a wise gardener, he clears the ground and prepares it for seed; but he finds the idle man already prepared, and he has scarcely the trouble of sowing; for vices, like weeds, need little fertilizing, except what the wind gives their ripe and winged seeds, shaking and scattering them all abroad. Indeed, lazy men may fitly be likened to a tropical prairie, over which the wind of temptation perpetually blows, drifting every vagrant seed from hedge and hill, and which — without a moment's rest through all the year — waves its rank harvest of luxuriant weeds.

First, the imagination will be haunted with unlawful visitants. Upon the outskirts of towns are shattered houses, abandoned by reputable people. They are not empty, because thieves, vagabonds and villains haunt them, in joint possession with rats, bats, and vermin. Such are idle men's imaginations — full of unlawful company.

The imagination is closely related to the passions, and fires them with its heat. The day-dreams of indolent youth, glow each hour with warmer colors, and bolder adventures. The imagination fashions scenes of enchantment, in which the passions revel; and it leads them out, in shadow at first, to deeds which soon they will seek in earnest. The brilliant colors of far-away clouds, are but the colors of the storm;

the evil day-dreams of indolent men, rosy at first and
distant, deepen every day, darker and darker, to the color of
actual evil. Then follows the blight of every habit.
Indolence promises, without redeeming the pledge; a mist
of forgetfulness rises up and obscures the memory of vows
and oaths. The negligence of laziness breeds more
falsehoods than the cunning of the swindler. As poverty
waits upon the steps of Indolence, so, upon such poverty,
brood equivocations, subterfuges, lying denials. Falsehood
becomes the instrument of every plan. Negligence of truth,
next occasional falsehood, then wanton mendacity — these
three traverse the whole road of lies.

Indolence as surely runs to dishonesty, as to lying.
Indeed, they are but different parts of the same road, and
not far apart. In directing the conduct of the Ephesian
converts, Paul says, "He who has been stealing must steal
no longer — but must work, doing something useful with
his own hands." The men who were thieves — were those
who had ceased to work. Industry was the road back to
honesty. When stores are robbed — the idle are first
suspected. The desperate forgeries and swindlings of past
years have taught men, upon their occurrence, to ferret their
authors among the unemployed, or among those vainly
occupied in wicked pleasures.

The terrible passion for stealing rarely grows upon the
young, except through the necessities of their idle
pleasures. Business is first neglected for amusement — and
amusement soon becomes the only business. The appetite
for wicked pleasure — outruns the means of procuring it.
The theater, the circus, the card-table, the midnight carouse
— all demand money. When scanty earnings are gone, the
young man pilfers from the til. First, because he hopes to
repay, and next, because he despairs of paying. For the

disgrace of stealing, ten dollars or a thousand will be the same — but not their respective pleasures. Next, he will gamble, since it is only another form of stealing. Gradually excluded from reputable society, the vagrant takes all the badges of vice, and is familiar with her paths; and, through them, enters the broad road of crime.

Society precipitates its lazy members, as water does its filth; and they form at the bottom, a pestilent sediment, stirred up by every breeze of evil, into riots, robberies and murders. Into it, drains all the filth — and out of it, as from a morass, flow all the streams of pollution. Brutal wretches, desperately hunted by the law, crawling in human filth, brood their villain schemes here, and plot mischief to man. Here resorts the violent demagogue, to stir up the putrid filth against his adversaries, or to bring up mobs out of this sea, which cannot rest — but casts up mire and dirt.

The results of Indolence upon communities, are as marked as upon individuals.

In a town of industrious people — the streets would be clean; houses neat and comfortable; fences in repair; school-houses swarming with rosy-faced children, decently clad, and well-behaved. The laws would be respected, because justly administered. The church would be thronged with devout worshipers. The tavern would be silent, and for the most part empty, or a welcome retreat for weary travelers. Liquor-sellers would fail — and mechanics grow rich. Labor would be honorable — and loafing a disgrace. For music, the people would have the blacksmith's anvil, and the carpenter's hammer; and at home, the spinning wheel, and girls cheerfully singing at their work. Debts would be seldom paid — because seldom made; but if contracted, no grim officer would be invited to the settlement. Town-officers would be respectable men, taking office reluctantly, and only for the public good. Public days would be full of sports, without fighting; and elections would be as orderly as weddings or funerals.

In a town of lazy men — I would expect to find crazy-houses, shingles and weather-boards knocked off; doors hingeless, and all a-creak: windows stuffed with rags, hats, or pillows. Instead of flowers in summer, and warmth in winter — every house would swarm with vermin in hot weather — and with starveling pigs in cold; fences would be curiosities of lazy contrivance, and gates hung with ropes, or lying flat in the mud. Lanky cattle would follow every loaded wagon, supplicating a morsel, with famine in their looks. Children would be ragged, dirty, brash. The school-house would be empty — and the jail full. The the church would be silent — and the taverns noisy. Lawyers would reign; constables flourish, and hunt sneaking criminals. The peace-officers would wink at tumults, arrest rioters in fun, and drink with them in good earnest. Good men would be obliged to keep hidden — and bad men would swear, fight, and rule the town. Public days would be scenes of confusion, and end in fights; elections would be drunken, illegal, boisterous and brutal.

The young abhor the last results of Idleness; but they do not perceive that the first steps lead to the last. They are in the opening of this career; but with them . . .

>it is genteel leisure — not laziness;
>it is relaxation — not sloth;
>it is amusement — not indolence.

But leisure, relaxation, and amusement, when men ought to be usefully engaged — are Indolence. A spurious

Industry — is the worst Idleness. A young man perceives that the first steps lead to the last — with everybody but himself! He sees others become drunkards by social tippling — he sips socially, as if he could not be a drunkard. He sees others become dishonest, by petty habits of fraud; but will indulge slight aberrations, as if he could not become thievish. Though others, by lying, lose all character — he does not imagine that his little dalliances with falsehood will make him a liar. He knows that indecent imaginations, immoral pictures, and illicit familiarities — have led thousands to the harlot's door, whose house is the way to Hell; yet he never sighs or trembles lest these things should take him to this inevitable way of damnation!

In reading these strictures upon Indolence, you will abhor it in others — without suspecting it in yourself! While you read, I fear you are excusing yourself! You are supposing that your leisure has not been laziness; or that, with your disposition, and in your circumstances — Indolence is harmless. Be not deceived! If you are idle — you are on the fast road to ruin — and there are few stopping places upon it. It is rather a precipice, than a road. While I point out the temptation to Indolence, scrutinize your course, and pronounce honestly upon your risk.

1. Some are tempted to Indolence by their wretched training — or rather, wretched lack of it. How many families are the most remiss — whose base condition and sufferings are the strongest inducement to Industry. The children have no inheritance — yet never work; they have no education — yet are never sent to school. It is hard to keep their rags around them — yet none of them will earn better clothing. If ever there was a case when a Government should interfere between parent and child —

that seems to be the one, where children are started in life with an education of vice! If, in every community, three things should be put together, which always work together — the front would be a tavern — the middle a jail — the rear a gallows — an infernal trinity! And the recruits for this three-headed monster, are largely drafted from the lazy children of worthless parents!

2. The children of rich parents are apt to be reared in Indolence. The ordinary motives to industry are lacking — and the temptations to sloth are multiplied. Other men labor to provide support; to secure homage; to obtain power; to multiply the elegant products of wealth. But the child of affluence inherits these things. Why should he labor — who may command universal service, whose money exhausts the luxuries of society, and makes rarities common by their abundance? Only the blind would not see, that riches and ruin run in one channel to prodigal children! The most rigorous regimen, the most confirmed industry, and steadfast morality — can alone disarm inherited wealth, and reduce it to a blessing.

The profligate wretch, who fondly watches his father's advancing decrepitude, and secretly curses the lingering steps of death, (seldom too slow except to hungry heirs,) at last is over-blessed in the tidings that the loitering death has come — and the estate is finally his. When the golden shower has fallen — he rules as a prince in a court of expectant parasites. All the sluices by which pleasurable vice drains an estate — are opened wide. A few years complete the ruin. The hopeful heir, avoided by all whom he has helped, ignorant of useful labor, and scorning a knowledge of it, fired with an incurable appetite for wicked excitement, sinks steadily down — a profligate, a wretch, a villain-scoundrel, a convicted felon! Let parents who hate their offspring — rear them to hate labor, and to inherit riches — and before long they will be stung by every vice, racked by its poison, and damned by its penalty!

3. Another cause of Idleness, is found in the secret effects of youthful indulgence. The purest pleasures lie within the circle of useful occupation. Mere pleasure — sought outside of usefulness — existing by itself — is fraught with poison! When its exhilaration has thoroughly kindled the mind, the passions thenceforth refuse a simple food; they crave and require an excitement, higher than any ordinary occupation can give. After reveling all night in wine-dreams, or amid the fascinations of the dance, or the deceptions of the drama — what does the dull store, or the dirty shop have — which can continue the pulse at this fever-heat of delight? The face of Pleasure to the youthful imagination — is the face of an angel, a paradise of smiles, a home of love; while the rugged face of Industry, embrowned by toil, is dull and repulsive: but at the end it is not so. These are harlot charms which Pleasure wears. At last, when Industry shall put on her beautiful garments, and rest in the palace which her own hands have built — Pleasure, blotched and diseased with indulgence, shall lie down and die upon the dunghill.

4. Bad example leads to Idleness. The children of industrious parents at the sight of vagrant rovers seeking their sports wherever they will — disrelish labor, and envy this unrestrained leisure. At the first relaxation of parental vigilance, they shrink from their odious tasks. Idleness is begun — when labor is a burden, and industry a bondage, and only idle relaxation a pleasure.

The example of famous people is not usually conducive to Industry. The idea insensibly fastens upon the mind, that greatness and hard labor are not companions. The inexperience of youth imagines that great men — are men of great leisure. They see them much in public, often applauded, and greatly followed. How disgusting in contrast is the mechanic's life; a tinkering shop — dark and smutty — is the only theater of his exploits; and labor, which covers him with sweat and fills him with weariness, brings neither notice nor praise. The ambitious apprentice, sighing over his soiled hands, hates his ignoble work — neglecting it, he aspires to better things — resorts to a bar-room; fights in a tavern; and dies in a ditch.

5. Men become Indolent through the reverses of fortune. Surely, despondency is a grievous thing, and a heavy load to bear. To see disaster and wreck in the present, and no light in the future; but only storms, ghastly by the contrast of past prosperity, and growing darker as they advance — to wear a constant expectation of woe like a belt; to see poverty at the door, imperiously knocking, while there is no strength to repel, or courage to bear its tyranny — indeed, this is dreadful enough!

But there is a thing more dreadful. It is more dreadful if the man is wrecked with his fortune. Can anything be more poignant in anticipation, than one's own self, unnerved, and helplessly drifting and driven down the troubled sea of life? Of all things on earth, next to his God, a broken man should cling to a courageous Industry. If it brings nothing back, and saves nothing — it will save him. To be pressed down by adversity has nothing in it of disgrace; but it is disgraceful to lie down under it like a scared dog. Indeed, to stand composedly in the storm, amidst its rage and wildest devastations; to let it beat over you, and roar around you, and pass by you, and leave you undismayed — this is to be a man.

Adversity is the mint in which God stamps upon us his image and superscription. In this matter, men may learn from insects. The ant will repair his dwelling as often as the mischievous foot crushes it; the spider will exhaust life itself, before he will live without a web; the bee can be decoyed from his labor neither by plenty nor scarcity. If summer is abundant, it toils none the less; if it be parsimonious of flowers, the tiny laborer sweeps a wider circle, and by Industry, repairs the frugality of the season. Man should be ashamed to be rebuked in vain by the spider, the ant, and the bee.

"Do you see a man diligent in his business? He will serve before kings; he will not serve before obscure men!"

Gamblers and Gambling

"When the soldiers had crucified Jesus, they divided his clothes among the four of them. They also took his robe, but it was seamless, woven in one piece from top to bottom. So they said, 'Rather than tearing it apart, let's cast dice for it!' So that is what they did." John 19:23-24

How marked in every age is a Gambler's character! The ferocious priesthood taunted Christ's dying agonies; the bewildered multitude, accustomed to cruelty, could shout; but no earthly creature — but a Gambler, could be so lost to all feeling as to sit down coolly under a dying man to wrangle for his garments, and arbitrate their avaricious differences by casting dice for his robe, with hands spotted with his spattered blood, warm and yet undried upon them! The descendants of these patriarchs of gambling, however, have taught us that there is nothing possible to Hell, uncongenial to these, its elect saints.

In this lecture, it is my disagreeable task to lead your steps down the dark path to their cruel haunts — there to exhibit their infernal passions, their awful ruin, and their ghastly memorials! In this house of darkness, amid fierce faces gleaming with the fire of fiercer hearts, amid oaths and groans and fiendish orgies, ending in murders and strewn with sweltering corpses — do not mistake, and suppose yourself in Hell — you are only in its precincts and vestibule!

Gambling is the staking or winning of property upon mere chance. The gardener renders produce, for his gains; the mechanic renders the product of labor and skill, for his gains; the gambler renders for his gain, the sleights of useless skill, or more often, downright cheating! Betting is gambling; there is no honest equivalent to its gains.

Dealings in speculative stocks are oftentimes sheer gambling, with all its worst evils. Profits so earned, are no better than the profits of dice, cards, or chance! When skill returns for its earnings a useful service, beneficial products, or profitable labor — it is honest commerce. The skill of a pilot in threading a narrow channel, the skill of a lawyer in threading a still more intricate one, are as substantial equivalents for a price received, as if they were merchant goods or agricultural products. But all gains of mere chance which result in no real benefit, are gambling gains.

Gaming, as it springs from a principle of our nature, has, in some form, probably existed in every age. We trace it in remote periods and among the most barbarous people. It loses none of its fascinations among a civilized people. On the contrary, the habit of fierce stimulants, the jaded appetite of luxury, and the satiety of wealth, seem to invite the master-excitant. Our land, not apt to be behind in good or evil, is full of gambling in all its forms — the gambling of commerce, the gambling of bets and wagers, and the gambling of games of chance. There is gambling in refined circles, and in the lowest; among the members of our national government, and of our state governments. Thief gambles with thief, in jail; the judge who sent them there, the lawyer who prosecuted, and the lawyer who defended them — often gamble too.

This vice, once almost universally prevalent among the Western legal system, and still too frequently disgracing its members, is, however, we are happy to believe, decreasing. In many circuits, not long ago, and in some now, the judge, the jury, and the bar, shuffled cards by night, and law by day — dealing out money and justice alike. The clatter of dice and cards disturbs your slumber on the boat, and rings drowsily from the upper rooms of the hotel. This vice pervades the city, extends over every line of travel, and infests the most moral districts. The secreted lamp, dimly lights the apprentices to their game; with unsuspected disobedience, boys creep out of their beds to it; it haunts the shop. The scoundrel in his lair, the scholar in his room; the pirate on his ship, mirthful women at parties; loafers in the street-corner, public leaders in their offices; the beggar under the hedge, the rascal in prison, and some professors of religion in the somnolent hours of the Sabbath — waste their energies by the ruinous excitement of the game!

Besides these players, there are troops of professional gamblers, troops of hangers-on, troops of youth to be drawn in. An inexperienced eye would detect in our peaceful towns, no signs of this vulture-flock — so in a sunny day, when all cheerful birds are singing merrily, not a buzzard can be seen; but let a carcass drop, and they will push forth their gaunt heads from their gloomy roosts, and come flapping from the dark woods to speckle the air, and dot the ground with their numbers!

The universal prevalence of this vice is a reason for parental vigilance; and a reason of remonstrance from the citizen, the parent, the minister of the gospel, the patriot, and the press. I propose to trace its beginning, describe its subjects, and detail its effects.

A young man, proud of freedom, anxious to exert his manhood, has tumbled his Bible, and sober books, and letters of counsel — into a dark closet. He has learned various accomplishments — to flirt, to boast, to swear, to fight, to drink. He has let every one of these chains be put around him, upon the solemn promise of Satan — that he would take them off whenever he wished. Hearing of the heroic feats of eminent gamblers — he emulates them. So, he ponders the game. He teaches what he has learned to his shopmates, and feels himself their master. As yet he has never played for stakes.

It begins thus: Peeping into a book-store, he watches until the sober customers go out; then slips in, and with assumed boldness, not concealing his shame — he asks for cards, buys them, and hastens out. The first game is to pay for the cards. After the relish of playing for a stake — no game can satisfy them without a stake. A few nuts are staked; then a bottle of wine; an oyster-supper. At last they can venture a sixpence in actual money — just for the amusement of it, of course. I need go no further — whoever wishes to do anything with the lad, can do it now. If properly plied, and gradually led — he will go to any length, and stop only at the gallows. Do you doubt it? Let us trace him a year or two further on.

With his father's blessing, and his mother's tears — the young man departs from home. He has received his patrimony, and embarks for life and independence. Upon his journey he rests at a city; visits the "school of morals;" lingers in more suspicious places; is seen by a sharper; and makes his acquaintance. The knave sits by him at dinner; gives him the news of the place, and a world of advice; cautions him against sharpers; inquires if he has money, and charges him to keep it secret; offers himself to make with him the rounds of the town, and secure him from imposition. At length, that he may see all, he is taken to a gaming-house — but, with apparent kindness, warned not to play. He stands by to see the various fortunes of the game; some, forever losing; some, touch what number they will, gaining piles of gold. Looking in thirst, where wine is free. A glass is taken; another of a better kind; next the best the landlord has, and two glasses of that.

A change comes over the youth; his exhilaration raises his courage — and lulls his caution. Gambling seen — seems a different thing from gambling painted by a pious father! Just then, his friend remarks that one might easily double his money by a few ventures — but that it was, perhaps, prudent not to risk. Only this was needed to fire his mind. What! only prudence between me and gain! Then that shall not be long! He stakes — he wins. Stakes again — he wins again. Glorious! I am the lucky man that is to break the bank! He stakes — and wins again. His pulse races; his face burns; his blood is up, and fear gone. He loses — loses again — loses all his winnings — loses more. But fortune turns again — he wins anew.

He has now lost all self-command. Gains excite him, and losses excite him more. He doubles his stakes; then trebles them — and all is swept away. He rushes on, puts up his whole purse — and loses the whole! Then he would borrow — but no man will lend. He is desperate, he will fight at a word. He is led to the street, and thrust out. The cool breeze which blows upon his fevered cheek, wafts the slow and solemn stroke of the clock — one — two — three — four; four of the morning!

Quick work of ruin! — an innocent man destroyed in a night! He staggers to his hotel, remembers as he enters it, that he has not even enough to pay his bill. It now flashes upon him that his friend, who never had left him for an hour before, had stayed behind where his money is, and, doubtless, is laughing over his spoils! His blood boils with rage.

But at length comes up the remembrance of home — a parent's training and counsels for more than twenty years, destroyed in a night! "Good God! what a wretch I have been! I am not fit to live. I cannot go home. I am a stranger here. Oh! that I were dead! Oh! that I had died before I knew this guilt, and were lying where my sister lies! Oh God! Oh God! my head will burst with agony!"

He stalks his lonely room with an agony which only the young heart knows in its first horrible awakening to remorse — when it looks despair full in the face, and feels its hideous incantations tempting him to suicide. Subdued at length by agony, cowed and weakened by distress — he is sought again by those who plucked him. Cunning to subvert inexperience, to raise the evil passions, and to allay the good — they make him their pliant tool.

Farewell, young man! I see your steps turned to that haunt again! I see hope lighting your face; but it is a lurid light, and never came from Heaven. Stop before that threshold! — turn, and bid farewell to home! — farewell to innocence! — farewell to venerable father and aged mother! — the next step shall part you from them all forever! And now henceforth be a mate to thieves — a brother to corruption. You have made a league with death — and unto death shall you go!

Let us here pause, to draw the likeness of a few who stand conspicuous in that vulgar crowd of gamblers, with which hereafter he will consort.

The first is a taciturn — a quiet man. No one knows when he comes into town, or when he leaves. No man hears of his gaining; for he never boasts, nor reports his luck. He spends little for parade; his money seems to go and come only through the game. He reads none, converses none, is neither a glutton nor a hard drinker; he sports few ornaments, and wears plain clothing. Upon the whole, he seems to be a gentlemanly man; and sober citizens say, "his only fault is gambling." What then is this "only fault?"

   In his heart, he has the most intense and consuming lust for gambling. He is quiet because every passion is absorbed in one; and that one burning at the highest flame. He thinks of nothing else — and cares only for this. All other things, even the hottest lusts of other men, are too cool to be temptations to him; so much deeper is the style of his passions. He will sit upon his chair, and no man shall see him move for hours, except to play his cards. He sees none come in — and none go out. Death might groan on one side of the room, and marriage might sport on the other — he would be aware of neither. Every other influence is shut out; one thing alone moves him — the game; and that leaves not one pulse of excitability unaroused — but stirs his soul to the very dregs!

   Very different is the roistering gamester. He bears a jolly face, a glistening eye something watery through watching and drink. His fingers are manacled in rings; his bosom glows with pearls and diamonds. He learns the time which he wastes, from a watch gorgeously carved, and slung around his neck by a ponderous golden chain. There is not as splendid a fellow to be seen sweeping through the streets. The landlord makes him welcome — he will pay his full bill. The tailor smiles like May — he will buy half his shop. Other places bid him welcome — he will bear large stealings.

Like the Judge, he makes his circuit — but not for justice; like the Preacher, he has his appointments — but not for instruction. His circuits are the race-courses, the crowded capital, days of general convocation, conventions, and mass-gatherings. He will flame on the race-track, bet his thousands, and beat the ring at swearing and oaths — vernacular, imported, simple, or compound. The drinking-booth smokes when he draws in his welcome suit. Did you see him only by day, flaming in apparel, jovial and free-hearted at the Restaurant or Hotel, you would think him a Prince let loose!

But night is his day. These are mere exercises, and brief prefaces to his real accomplishments. He is keen indeed — who is sharper than he is. No one is quicker, slyer, and more alert at a game. He can shuffle the pack until an honest man would as soon think of looking for a particular drop of water in the ocean — as for a particular card in any particular place. Perhaps he is ignorant which is at the top and which at the bottom! At any rate, watch him closely, or you will get a lean hand — and he a fat one. A plain man would think him a wizard — or the devil. When he touches a pack they seem alive, and acting to his will, rather than his touch. He deals them like lightning, they rain like snow-flakes, sometimes one, sometimes two, if need be four or five together, and his hand hardly moved. If he loses, very well, he laughs; if he gains, he only laughs a little more. Full of stories, full of songs, full of wit, full of roistering spirit — yet do not trespass too much upon his good nature with insult! All this outside is only the spotted hide which covers the tiger! He who provokes this man, shall see what lightning can break out of a summer-seeming cloud!

These do not fairly represent the race of gamblers — conveying too favorable an impression. There is one, often met on Steam-boats, traveling solely to gamble. He has the servants, or steward, or some partner, in league with him, to fleece every unwary player whom he inveigles to a game. He deals falsely; heats his dupe to madness by drink, drinking none himself; watches the signal of his accomplice telegraphing his opponent's hand; at a stray look, he will slip your money off and steal it. To cover false playing, or to get rid of paying losses — he will lie fiercely, and swear uproariously, and break up the play to fight with knife or pistol — first scraping the table of every penny.

When the passengers are asleep, he surveys the luggage, to see what may be worth stealing; he pulls a watch from under the pillow of one sleeper; fumbles in the pockets of another; and gathers booty throughout the cabin. Leaving the boat before morning, he appears at some village hotel — a magnificent gentleman, a polished traveler, or even a distinguished nobleman!

There is another gambler, cowardly, sleek, stealthy, humble, mousing, and mean — a simple blood-sucker. For money, he will be a tool to other gamblers. He will steal for them — and from them. He plays the jackal, and searches victims for them, humbly satisfied to pick the bones afterward. Thus, (to employ his own language,) he ropes in the inexperienced young, flatters them, teaches them, inflames their passions, purveys to their appetites, cheats them, debauches them, draws them down to his own level — and then lords it over them in malignant baseness. Himself impure, he plunges others into lasciviousness; and with a train of reeking accomplices, he revolves a few years in the orbit of the game, the brothel, and the doctor's shop — and then sinks and dies. The world is then purer, and good men thank God that he is gone.

Besides these, time would fail me to describe the ineffable dignity of a gambling judge; the cautious, phlegmatic lawyer, gambling from sheer avarice; the broken-down and cast-away politician, seeking in the game the needed excitement, and a fair field for all the base tricks he once played off as a patriot; the pert, sharp, keen, jockey-gambler; the soaked, obese, plethoric, wheezing, bacchanal; and a crowd of ignoble worthies, wearing all the badges and titles of vice, throughout its base peerage.

A detail of the evils of gambling should be preceded by an illustration of that constitution of mind out of which they mainly spring — I mean its Excitability. The body is not stored with a fixed amount of strength, nor the mind with a uniform measure of excitement; but both are capable, by stimulation, of expansion of strength or feeling, almost without limit. Experience shows, that within certain bounds, excitement is healthful and necessary — but beyond this limit, exhausting and destructive. Men are allowed to choose between moderate but long-continued excitement — and intense but short-lived excitement. Too generally they prefer the latter.

To gain this intense thrill, a thousand methods are tried. The inebriate obtains it by drink and drugs; the politician, by the keen interest of the civil campaign; the young by amusements which violently inflame and gratify their appetites. When once this higher flavor of stimulus has been tasted, all that is less — becomes vapid and disgustful.

A sailor tries to live on shore — a few weeks suffice. To be sure, there is no hardship, or cold, or suffering; but neither is there the strong excitement of the ocean, the gale, the storm, and the world of strange sights. The politician perceives that his private affairs are deranged, his family neglected, his character aspersed, his feelings exacerbated. When men hear him confess that his career is a hideous waking dream, the race vexatious, and the end vanity — they wonder that he clings to it; but he knows that nothing but the fiery wine which he has tasted, will rouse up that intense excitement, now become necessary to his happiness. For this reason, great men often cling to public office with all its envy, jealousy, care, toil, hates, competitions, and unrequited fidelity; for these very disgusts, and the perpetual struggle — strike a deeper chord of excitement than is possible to the gentler touches of home, friendship and love.

Here too is the key to the real evil of promiscuous novel-reading, to the habit of reverie and mental romancing. None of life's common duties can excite to such wild pleasure as these; and they must be continued, or the mind reacts into the lethargy of fatigue and boredom.

It is upon this principle, that men love pain; suffering is painful to a spectator; but in tragedies, at public executions, at boxing matches, at cock-fightings, horse-races, dog-baitings, bull-fights, gladiatorial shows — pain excites a jaded mind as nothing else can. A tyrant torments for the same reason that a girl reads her tear-bedewed romance, or an inebriate drinks his beer. No longer susceptible even to inordinate stimuli — actual moans, and shrieks, and the writhing of utter agony — just suffice to excite his worn-out sense, and inspire, probably, less emotion than ordinary men have in listening to a tragedy or reading a bloody novel.

Gambling is founded upon the very worst perversion of this powerful element of our nature. It heats every part of the mind like an oven. The faculties which produce calculation, pride of skill, of superiority, love of gain, hope, fear, jealousy, hatred — are absorbed in the game, and exhilarated, or exacerbated by victory or defeat. These passions are, doubtless, excited in men by the daily occurrences of life; but then they are transient, and counteracted by a thousand grades of emotion, which rise and fall like the undulations of the sea. But in gambling there is no intermission, no counteraction. The whole mind is excited to the utmost, and concentrated at its extreme point of excitation for hours and days, with the additional waste of sleepless nights, profuse drinking, and other congenial immoralities. Every other pursuit becomes tasteless; for no ordinary duty has in it, a stimulus which can scorch a mind which now refuses to burn without blazing, or to feel an interest which is not intoxication.

The victim of excitement is like a mariner who ventures into the edge of a whirlpool for a motion more exhilarating than plain sailing. He is unalarmed during the first few gyrations, for escape is easy. But each turn sweeps him further in; the power augments, the speed becomes terrific as he rushes toward the vortex; all escape now hopeless. A noble ship went in; it is spit out in broken fragments, splintered spars, crushed masts, and cast up for many a rood along the shore.

The specific evils of gambling may now be almost imagined.

1. Gambling diseases the mind, unfitting it for the duties of life. Gamblers are seldom industrious men in any useful vocation. A gambling mechanic finds his labor less relishing — as his passion for play increases. He grows unsteady, neglects his work, becomes unfaithful to promises; and what he does perform, he slights. Little jobs seem little enough; he desires immense contracts, whose uncertainty has much the excitement of gambling — and for the best of reasons; and in the pursuit of great and sudden profits, by wild schemes — he stumbles over into ruin, leaving all who employed or trusted him, in the rubbish of his speculations.

A gambling lawyer, neglecting the drudgery of his profession, will court its exciting duties. To explore authorities, compare reasons, digest, and write — this is tiresome. But to advocate, to engage in fiery contests with keen opponents, this is nearly as good as gambling. Many a ruined client has cursed the law, and cursed a stupid jury, and cursed everybody for his irretrievable loss — except his lawyer, who gambled all night when he should have prepared the case, and came half asleep and debauched into court in the morning to lose a good case mismanaged, and snatched from his gambling hands, by the art of sober opponents.

A gambling student, if such a thing can be, withdraws from thoughtful authors — to the brilliant and spicy; from the pure among these — to the sharp and ribald; from all reading about depraved life — to seeing; from sight — to experience. Gambling vitiates the imagination, corrupts the tastes, destroys the industry — for no man will drudge for cents, who gambles for dollars by the hundred; or practice a piddling economy, while, with almost equal indifference, he makes or loses five hundred in a night.

2. For a like reason, gambling destroys all domestic habits and affections. Home is a prison to an inveterate gambler; there is no air there that he can breathe. For a moment he may sport with his children, and smile upon his wife; but his heart, its strong passions, are not there. A little rill of his affections may flow through the family — but the deep river flows away from home. On the outcome of a game, Tacitus narrates that the ancient Germans would stake their property, their wives, their children, and themselves! What less than this is it, when a man will stake that property which is to give his family bread, and that honor which gives them place and rank in society?

When playing becomes desperate gambling, the heart is a hearth where all the fires of gentle feelings have smouldered to ashes; and a thorough-paced gamester could rattle dice in a charnel-house, and wrangle for his stakes amid murder, and pocket gold dripping with the blood of his own kindred!

3. Gambling is the parent and companion of every vice which pollutes the heart, or injures society. It is a practice so disallowed among Christians, and so excluded by mere moralists, and so hateful to industrious and thriving men — that those who practice it are shut up to themselves. Unlike lawful pursuits, it is not modified or restrained by collision with others. Gamblers herd with gamblers. They tempt and provoke each other to all evil, without affording one restraint, and without providing the counterbalance of a single virtuous impulse. They are like snakes coiling among snakes — poison and poisoning! They are like plague-patients — infected and diffusing infection; each sick, and all contagious! It is impossible to put bad men together — and not have them grow worse. The herding of convicts promiscuously, produced such a fermentation of

depravity, that, long ago, legislators forbade it. When criminals, out of jail, herd together by choice — the same corrupt nature will doom them to growing loathsomeness, because to increasing wickedness.

    4. Gambling is a provocative of alcohol. The bottle is almost as needful as the card, the ball, or the dice. Some are seduced to drink; some drink for imitation, at first, and fashion. When super-excitements, at intervals, subside, their victim cannot bear the deathlike gloom of the reaction; and, by drugs or liquor, wind up their system to the glowing point again. Therefore, drinking is the invariable concomitant of the theater, circus, race-course, gaming-table, and of all amusements which powerfully excite all but the moral feelings. When the double fires of dice and brandy blaze under a man — he will soon be consumed. If men are found who do not drink, they are the more noticeable, because they are exceptions.

    5. Gambling is, even in its fairest form, the almost inevitable cause of dishonesty. Robbers have robbers' honor; thieves have thieves' law; and pirates conform to pirates' regulations. But where is there a gambler's code? One law there is, and this not universal — pay your gambling debts. But on the wide question, how is it fair to cheat — what law is there? What will shut a man out from a gambler's club? May he not discover his opponent's hand by fraud? May not a concealed thread, pulling the significant one — or the sign of a bribed servant or waiter, inform him, and yet his standing be fair? May he not cheat in shuffling, and yet be in full orders and accepted? May he not cheat in dealing, and yet be a welcome gambler? May he not steal the money from your pile by laying his hands upon it, just as any other thief would — and yet be an

approved gambler? May not the whole code be stated thus — get what you can, and in any way you can!

I am told, perhaps, that there are honest gamblers, gentlemanly gamblers. Certainly; there are always ripe apples — before there are rotten! Men always begin — before they end; there is always an approximation, before there is contact. Players will play truly — until they get used to playing untruly. They will be honest — until they cheat. They will be honorable — until they become base. And when you have said all this, what does it amount to but this — that men who really gamble, really cheat; and that they only do not cheat, who are not yet real gamblers? If this mends the matter — let it be so amended.

I have spoken of gamesters only among themselves; this is the least part of the evil; for who is concerned when lions destroy bears, or wolves devour wolf-cubs, or snakes sting vipers?

In respect to that department of gambling which includes the roping-in of strangers, young men, collecting-clerks, and unsuspecting green-hands — and robbing them, I have no language strong enough to mark down its turpitude, its infernal rapacity! After hearing many of the scenes familiar to every gambler, I think Satan might be proud of their dealings, and look up to them with that deferential respect, with which one monster gazes upon a superior. There is not even the expectation of honesty.

Some scullion-herald of iniquity decoys the unwary wretch into the secret room; he is tempted to drink; made confident by the specious simplicity of the game; allowed to win; and every bait and lure and blind is employed — then he is plucked to the skin by tricks which appear as fair as honesty itself. The robber avows his deed, does it openly; the gambler sneaks to the same result under skulking pretenses.

There is a frank way, and a mean way of doing a wicked thing. The gambler takes the meanest way of doing the dirtiest deed. The victim's own partner is sucking his blood; it is a league of sharpers, to get his money at any rate; and the wickedness is so unblushing and unmitigated, that it gives, at last, an instance of what the deceitful human heart, knavish as it is — is ashamed to try to cover or conceal; but confesses with helpless honesty, that it is fraud, cheating, stealing, robbery — and nothing else.

If I walk the dark street, and a perishing, hungry wretch meets me and bears off my purse with but a single dollar, the whole town awakes; the officers are alert, the myrmidons of the law scout, and hunt, and bring in the trembling culprit to stow him in the jail. But a worse thief may meet me, decoy my steps, and by a greater dishonesty, filch ten thousand dollars — and what then? The story spreads, the sharpers move abroad unharmed, no one stirs! It is the day's conversation; and like a sound, it rolls to the distance, and dies in an echo.

Shall such astounding iniquities be vomited out amidst us — and no man care? Do we love our children — and yet let them walk in a den of vipers? Shall we pretend to virtue, and purity, and religion — and yet make partners of our social life, men whose heart has conceived such damnable deeds, and whose hands have performed them? Shall there be even in the eye of religion, no difference between the corrupter of youth and their guardian? Are all the lines and marks of morality so effaced, is the nerve and courage of virtue so quailed by the frequency and boldness of flagitious crimes — that men, covered over with wickedness, shall find their iniquity no obstacle to their advancement among a Christian people!

In almost every form of iniquity, there is some shade or trace of good. But we have in gambling, a crime standing alone — dark, malignant, uncompounded wickedness! It seems in its full growth, to be a monster without a tender mercy, devouring its own offspring without one feeling but appetite!

A gamester, as such, is the cool, calculating, essential spirit of concentrated avaricious selfishness. His intellect is a living thing, quickened with double life for villainy; his heart is steel of fourfold temper. When a man begins to gamble, he is as a noble tree full of sap, green with leaves — a shade to beasts, and a covert to birds. When one becomes a thorough gambler, he is like that tree lightning-smitten, rotten in root, dry in branch, and sapless; seasoned hard and tough; nothing lives beneath it, nothing on its branches, unless a hawk or a vulture perches for a moment to whet its beak, and fly screaming away for its prey.

To every young man who indulges in the least form of gambling, I raise a warning voice! Under the specious name of Amusement — you are laying the foundation of gambling! Playing is the seed which comes up gambling. It is the light wind which brings up the storm. It is the white frost which preludes the winter. You are mistaken, however, in supposing that it is harmless in its earliest beginnings. Its terrible blight belongs, doubtless, to a later stage; but its consumption of time, its destruction of industry, its distaste for the calmer pleasures of life — belong to the very beginning. You will begin to play with every generous feeling. Amusement will be the plea. At the beginning the game will excite enthusiasm, pride of skill, the love of mastery, and the love of money. The love of money, at first almost imperceptible, at last will rule out all the rest — like Aaron's rod — a serpent, swallowing every other serpent! Generosity, enthusiasm, pride and skill, love of mastery — will be absorbed in one mighty feeling — the savage lust of filthy lucre!

There is a downward climax in this sin. The opening and ending are fatally connected, and drawn toward each other with almost irresistible attraction. If gambling is a vortex — then playing is the outer ring of the maelstrom. The thousand pound stake, the whole estate put up on a game — what are these but the instruments of kindling that tremendous excitement which a diseased heart craves? What is the amusement for which you play — but the excitement of the game? And for what but excitement — does the jaded gambler play? You differ from him only in the degree of the same feeling.

Do not solace yourself that you shall escape because others have; for they stopped, and you go on. Are you as safe as they, when you are in the gulf-stream of perdition — and they on the shore?

But have you ever asked, how many have escaped? Not one in a thousand is left unblighted! You have nine hundred and ninety-nine chances against you — and one for you; and will you go on? If a disease should stalk through the town, devouring whole families, and sparing only one in five hundred — would you lie down under it quietly because you had one chance in five hundred? Had a scorpion stung you, would it alleviate your pangs to reflect that you had only one chance in one hundred in surviving? Had you swallowed corrosive poison, would it ease your convulsions to think there was only one chance in fifty for you? I do not call every man who plays a gambler — but a gambler in embryo.

Let me trace your course from the amusement of innocent playing — to its almost inevitable end.

First Scene. A genteel coffee-house — whose humane screen conceals a line of alcohol bottles, and hides respectable blushes from impertinent eyes. There is a quiet little room opening out of the bar; and here sit four jovial youths. The cards are out — the wines are in. The fourth is a reluctant hand; he does not love the drink, nor approve the game. He anticipates and fears the result of both. Why is he here? He is a whole-souled fellow, and is afraid to seem ashamed of any fashionable gaiety. He will sip his wine upon the importunity of a friend newly come to town, and is too polite to spoil that friend's pleasure by refusing a part in the game.

They sit, shuffle, deal; the night wears on, the clock telling no tale of passing hours — the prudent liquor-fiend has made it safely dumb. The night is getting old; its dank air grows fresher; the east is grey; the gaming and drinking and hilarious laughter are over, and the youths wending homeward. What says conscience? No matter what it says; they did not hear — and we will not. Whatever was said, it was very shortly answered thus: "This has not been gambling; all were gentlemen; there was no cheating; simply a convivial evening; no stakes except the bills incident to the entertainment. If anybody blames a young man for a little innocent exhilaration on a special occasion, he is a superstitious bigot; let him croak!" Such a garnished game is made the text to justify the whole round of gambling. Let us, then, look at the

Second Scene. In a room so silent that there is no sound except the shrill rooster crowing the morning, where the forgotten candles burn dimly over the long and lengthened wick, sit four men. Carved marble could not be more motionless, save their hands. Pale, watchful, though weary, their eyes pierce the cards, or furtively read each other's faces. Hours have passed over them thus. At length they rise without words; some, with a satisfaction which only makes their faces brightly haggard, scrape off the piles of money; others, dark, sullen, silent, fierce — move away from their lost money. The darkest and fiercest of the four is that young friend who only sat down to make up enough players for a game! He will never sit so innocently again. What says he to his conscience now! I have a right to gamble; I have a right to be damned too, if I choose; whose business is it?

Third Scene. Years have passed on. He has seen youth ruined, at first with expostulation, then with only silent regret, then consenting to take part of the spoils; and finally, he has himself decoyed, duped, and stripped them without mercy. Go with me into that dilapidated house, not far from the landing, at New Orleans. Look into that dirty room. Around a broken table, sitting upon boxes, kegs, or rickety chairs — see a filthy crew dealing cards smudged with tobacco, grease and liquor. One has a pirate-face burnished and burnt with brandy; a shock of grizzly, matted hair, half covering his villain eyes, which glare out like a wild beast's from a thicket. Close by him wheezes a white-faced, dropsical wretch, vermin-covered, and stenchful. A scoundrel-Spaniard, and a burly negro, (the jolliest of the four,) complete the group. They have spectators — drunken sailors, and ogling, thieving, drinking women, who should have died long ago, when all that was womanly died.

Here hour draws on hour, sometimes with brutal laughter, sometimes with threat, and oath, and uproar. The last few stolen dollars lost, and temper too, each charges each with cheating, and high words ensue, and blows; and the whole gang burst out the door, beating, biting, scratching, and rolling over and over in the dirt and dust. The worst, the fiercest, the drunkest, of the four — is our friend who began by sitting down to make up enough players for a game!

Fourth Scene. Upon this bright day, stand with me, if you would be sick of humanity, and look over that multitude of men kindly gathered to see a murderer hung! At last, a guarded cart drags on a thrice-guarded wretch. At the gallows' ladder, his courage fails. His coward-feet refuse to ascend. Dragged up, he is supported by bustling officials; his brain reels, his eye swims, while the meek minister utters a final prayer by his leaden ear. The prayer is said, the noose is fixed, the signal is given; a shudder runs through the crowd as he swings through the air. After a moment, his convulsed limbs stretch down, and hang heavily and still; and he who began to gamble to make up enough players for a game, and ended with stabbing an enraged victim whom he had fleeced — has here played his last game — himself the stake!

I feel impelled, in closing, to call the attention of all sober citizens to some potent influences which are exerted in favor of gambling.

In our civil economy we have Legislators to devise and enact wholesome laws; Lawyers to counsel and aid those who need the laws' relief; and Judges to determine and administer the laws. If Legislators, Lawyers, and Judges are gamblers — with what hope do we warn off the young from this deadly fascination, against such authoritative examples of high public functionaries? With what eminent fitness does that Judge press the bench, who in private commits the vices which officially he is set to condemn! With what singular terrors does he frown on a convicted gambler, with whom he played last night, and will play again tonight! How wisely should the fine be light, which the sprightly criminal will win and pay out of the Judge's own pocket!

With the name of Judge — is associated ideas of immaculate purity, sober piety, and fearless, strict justice. Let it then be counted a dark crime for a recreant official so far to forget his revered place, and noble office, as to run the gauntlet of filthy vices, and make the word Judge, to suggest an incontinent trifler, who smites with his mouth, and smirks with his eye; who holds the rod to strike the criminal, and smites only the law — to make a gap for criminals to pass through! If God loves this land — may he save it from truckling, drinking, swearing, gambling, wicked Judges!

With such Judges I must associate corrupt Legislators, whose bawling patriotism leaks out in all the sinks of infamy at the Capital. These living exemplars of vice, pass still-born laws against vice. Are such men sent to the Capital only to practice debauchery? Laborious seedsmen — they gather every germ of evil; and laborious sowers — at home they strew them far and wide! It is a burning shame, a high outrage, that public men, by corrupting the young with the example of manifold vices — should pay back their constituents for their honors!

Our land has little to fear from abroad — and much from within. We can bear foreign aggression, scarcity, the losses of commerce, plagues, and pestilences; but we cannot bear wicked Judges, corrupt Courts, gambling Legislators, and a wicked, corrupt, and gambling constituency! Let us not be deceived! The decay of civil institutions, begins at the core. The outside wears all the lovely hues of ripeness, when the inside is rotting. Decline does not begin in bold and startling acts; but, as in autumnal leaves, in rich and glowing colors. Over diseased vitals, consumptive laws wear the hectic blush, a brilliant eye, and transparent skin. Could the public sentiment declare that Personal Morality is the first element of patriotism; that corrupt Legislators are the most pernicious of criminals; that the Judge who lets the villain off, is the villain's patron; that tolerance of crime is intolerance of virtue — our nation might defy all enemies and live forever!

And now, my young friends, I beseech you to let alone this evil, before it is meddled with. You are safe from vice — when you avoid even its appearance; and only then. The first steps to wickedness are imperceptible! We do not wonder at the inexperience of Adam; but it is wonderful that six thousand years' repetition of the same arts, and the same uniform disaster — should have taught men nothing! that generation after generation should perish, and the wreck be no warning!

The mariner searches his chart for hidden rocks, stands off from perilous shoals, and steers wide of reefs on which hang shattered morsels of wrecked ships. But the mariner upon life's sea, carries no chart of other men's voyages, drives before every wind that will speed him, draws upon horrid shores with slumbering crew, or heads in upon roaring reefs — as though he would not perish where thousands have perished before him!

Hell is populated with the victims of harmless amusements! Will men never learn, that the way to Hell is through the Valley of Deceit! The power of Satan to hold his victims, is nothing to that mastery of art by which he first gains them. When he approaches to charm us, it is not as a grim fiend, gleaming from a ghastly cloud — but as an angel of light radiant with innocence. His words fall like dew upon the flower; as musical as the crystal-drop warbling from a fountain. Beguiled by his deceits, he leads you to the enchanted ground. Oh! how it glows with every refulgent hue of Heaven! Afar off, he marks the dismal gulf of vice and crime; its smoke of torment slowly rising, and rising forever! and he himself cunningly warns you of its dread disaster, for the very purpose of blinding and drawing you there! He leads you to captivity through all the bowers of lulling magic. He plants your foot near fragrant flowers; he fans your cheek with balmy breath; he overhangs your head with rosy clouds; he fills your ear with distant, drowsy music, charming every sense to rest.

Oh you, who have thought the way to Hell was as bleak and frozen as the Arctic, as parched and barren as the Sahara, strewed like Golgotha with bones and skulls, reeking with stench like the valley of Gehenna — witness your mistake! The way to Hell looks pleasant! It is a broad highway; no lion is there, no ominous bird to hoot a warning, no echoings of the wailing-pit, no lurid gleams of distant fires, or moaning sounds of hidden woe! Paradise is imitated — to build you a way to death; the flowers of Heaven are stolen and poisoned; the sweet plant of knowledge is here; the pure white flower of religion; seeming virtue and the charming tints of innocence are scattered all along like native herbage. The enchanted victim travels on. Standing afar behind, and from a silver trumpet, a heavenly messenger sends down the wind a solemn warning: "There is a way which seems right to man — but the end thereof is death!" And again, with louder blast: "The wise man foresees the danger and takes refuge; but fools goes blindly on and suffer the consequences!"

Startled for a moment, the victim pauses; gazes around upon the flowery scene, and whispers, Is it not harmless? — "Harmless," responds a serpent from the grass! — "Harmless," echo the sighing winds! — Harmless," re-echo a hundred airy tongues! If now a gale from Heaven might only sweep the clouds away through which the victim gazes; oh! if God would break that potent spell which chains the blasts of Hell, and let the sulphur-stench roll up the valley, how would the vision change! — the road would become a track of dead men's bones! — the heavens a lowering storm! — the balmy breezes, distant wailings — and all those balsam-shrubs that lied to his senses, sweat drops of blood upon their poison-boughs!

You who are meddling with the edges of vice, you are on this road — and utterly duped by its enchantments! Your eye has already lost its honest glance, your taste has lost its purity, your heart throbs with poison! The leprosy is all over you, its blotches and eruptions cover you. Your feet stand on slippery places, whence in due time they shall slide, if you refuse the warning which I raise. They shall slide from Heaven, never to be visited by a gambler; slide down to that fiery abyss below you, out of which none ever come!

Then, when the last card is cast, and the game over, and you lost; then, when the echo of your fall shall ring through hell — in malignant triumph, shall the Arch-Gambler, who cunningly played for your soul, have his prey! Too late you shall look back upon life as a Mighty Game, in which you were the stake, and Satan the winner!

Made in United States
Orlando, FL
05 December 2022